THE
END OF
AMERICA

100 DAYS
THAT SHOOK THE WORLD

J.J. SEFTON

THE
END OF
AMERICA

100 DAYS
THAT SHOOK THE WORLD

Published by

 **CALAMO**

The Calamo Press
Washington D.C.

calamopress.com
Currente-Calamo LLC
455 Massachusetts Ave., NW, #216
Washington, DC 20001
© Copyright by J.J. Sefton
All rights reserved

ISBN: 978-1-7351928-4-0

Cover artwork by Sabo

To my parents, of blessed memory, who gave me everything.

Dad. Artistic talent, cornball humor, Gershwin,
a sunny disposition no matter what...
Mom. Shoah survivor, a dry wit, a passion for the English
language, indomitable courage...

FOREWORD

By Benjamin Braddock

"There are decades where nothing happens; and there are weeks where decades happen." — Vladimir Ilyich Lenin.

Only 100 days, but they were filled with happenings that would normally take a much longer time to unfold. For decades we have been proverbial frogs in the pot, with the heat increasing at such a slow pace that it went almost unnoticed. But the regime change we just witnessed was like detonating a thermonuclear bomb under the pot. This diary of the first 100 days of the Biden regime captures a valuable historical perspective — that of an intelligent dissident experiencing as it unfolded day by day, with all the turbulent emotions of reacting in realtime — rather than a retrospective account written when all of the connections could be fitted into a single overarching narrative. There is little I could add to the author's incisive commentary on the first hundred days, so I will just relate my own experience of the events leading up to Day 1.

As we entered the homestretch of President Trump's re-election campaign, things were feeling great. Trump had very decisively defeated the lab-engineered virus. While in reality his condition had been quite severe, to the public, he had

1

made it look easy. Always the showman, he returned to the White House as a conquering hero, ripping off his mask and saluting before going inside for a dexamethasone-induced manic tweeting spree. How can you not love the guy? From that point on, you could feel the energy mounting. People in the inner-suburbs started putting up American flags (the alternative to putting up an actual Trump yard sign for those who didn't want their house vandalized by the DNC's Antifa shock troops), in the outer suburbs and rural areas the visible support for Trump was completely unlike anything I've seen in decades. There were car parades that stretched for miles, boat parades that rivaled the Spanish Armada, the campaign had a festive carnival atmosphere that mirrored the kind of joyous electioneering you see in Latin America (incidentally, the most overlooked factor in Trump's success among Latinos was that his campaign was **fun**). His rallies were huge and manic, and social media was completely dominated by his online soldiers.

Aside from feeling, we also had hard data that showed the narrative being pushed by the mainstream media and their pollsters was completely false. Using polls showing Biden ahead by ~10-20 points in the Rust Belt and ~5 points in red states like Texas, they had built a narrative that Biden was inevitable. But we knew those polls were dead wrong. After the the Summer of Carnage that saw Trump supporters being murdered and bloodied in the streets and republican senators attacked by mobs as they left the Republican National Convention, there wasn't a Trump voter within 100 miles of a city who was going to tell a stranger over the phone who they were actually voting for. To overcome this issue, Trafalgar Group, Richard Baris, and Rasmussen polling all developed methodology which allowed for polling the election accurately by giving the respondent ways to signal support for Trump while maintaining good opsec. These polls showed Trump was well on his way to a 300+ electoral college win. We also knew going into the final weekend of the campaign that Democrats were well behind their 2016 early vote lead in Arizona, Florida, North Carolina, Wisconsin, and Michigan. Republicans actually beat the Democrats in early voting returns in Michigan and Wisconsin by 2 and 6 points, respectively. We knew this not because of polling — which predicted a wide preference for Biden among early voters (in the same polls that showed him winning Wisconsin and Michigan by 20 and Texas by 5) — but by looking at the reports from state officials which showed the partisan breakdown of voters who had voted early or returned a mail-in ballot. The only state that showed Democrats anywhere near their early voting target was Pennsylvania, but not by enough to overcome Trump's in-person vote.

Although things looked and felt great on the surface, I couldn't shake my sense of uneasiness and suspicion. Media spin aside, the people running Biden's campaign staff were seasoned and serious, completely unlike the delusional and incompetent sycophants who ran Hillary's 2016 campaign. Surely they knew what the polling and early vote numbers indicated even if they had somehow missed the energy on the ground. Why wasn't Biden out campaigning like he had an election to win? He was spending more days at home than he was on the campaign trail. Something wasn't right.

Along with my gut feeling, there were several clear indicators that a psyop was underway. Major media outlets had been saying for months that this election was going to cause a lot of confusion and chaos because the in-person votes (expected to go for Trump) would be counted earlier in the night, giving Trump the appearance of a lead, which would vanish when the early votes (expected to go for Biden) were finally counted and reported. They were already running predictive programming on the public for the operation that was about to be carried out. And this was not something the media cooked up on it's own, far from it. They were just running the narrative that was given them by a shadowy organization known as the Transition Integrity Project. The idea that there would be a significant split in the early vote and election day vote was seeded in June 2020, long before voters even considered whether they would be voting early or in-person. As they put it, "The concept of "election night," is no longer accurate and indeed is dangerous."

In September, The Atlantic ran an article on what would happen if Trump successfully challenged voter fraud and excluded illegal ballots from counting, in it they said "The intent on the left, if it comes to that, is to meet Trump's demonstrators with overwhelming numbers; the goal is to establish a presence more reminiscent of... the more recent prodemocracy protests in Ukraine and Hong Kong, than of anything in modern American experience." In other words, the CIA's color revolution playbook was about to come home to America. Those of us in the Trump campaign orbit were preparing for significant fraud as well as a prolonged occupation of DC by Antifa and the lumpenprole mob. But we assumed that those further up the campaign hierarchy were making similar preparations. After all, Trump had been warning of fraud for months. Surely the top guys had built out a robust operation to ensure the integrity of the vote. In other words, I felt that the shenanigans would be like 2016's shenanigans on steroids but have the same end result. I was wrong.

Election night, 7:01pm EST. My first indicator that something was afoot was that 1 minute after polls had closed in Virginia, the state had been called for Biden. Weird. The state had only gone for Hillary by 5 points back in 2016, despite Trump's state campaign there very publicly imploding and being disbanded a month before the election. This election was different. Trump's Virginia team had run a solid campaign, there was widespread discontent over Covid restrictions, and internal polling had him within the margin of error. Surely they would wait for some results before calling the race.

Well, results from Virginia did start to come in. And they signaled something shocking. He was over-performing at a level his state campaign had not even mapped out. I thought "If he's doing this well in a state they called for Biden before any votes were in, he's going to absolutely clean-up the battlegrounds." Sure enough, North Carolina and Florida began to report and they showed a red wave of epic proportions. We had lost Miami-Dade County by 30 points back in 2016. Now we were winning it outright (final Miami numbers: 24 point shift to Trump in 4 years). GNow Ohio comes in, we flip the working-class Democratic bastion of Mahoning County, Trump is running 7 to 14 points ahead of his 2016 margin. Wisconsin starts reporting, we flipped Kenosha County. We're up big in Georgia, Pennsylvania, Michigan, Wisconsin. Nevada and Arizona are looking tight but solid.

And then, something happened.

With hundreds of thousands of votes left to count, Fox News calls Arizona for Biden. WTF? Twitter catches on fire, "Are these people insane?" It was like complete unreality. The liberal networks, AP, New York Times, all of them had Arizona as too close to call. Fox was the President's network. Were these people on drugs or something? Oh well, it'll be retracted like Florida in 2000.

Minutes tick by. Refresh. 10 minutes. Refresh. 20 minutes. Refresh. 30 minutes. Refresh. What's happening? Why aren't the vote counts being updated? Trump is still leading in Virginia, looks like Republicans are picking up several house seats there. Looks like a GOP trifecta in House, Senate, and White House. Uh oh, 200,000 votes just got reported in Fairfax County. 99% of them are for Biden. Still no more votes reported from the battlegrounds. Hours creep by. Trump briefly appears and rambles. Still no updates from

Georgia, Wisconsin, Michigan, Pennsylvania, Arizona, or Nevada. It's late, I need to be in fighting shape the next day so I go to bed. Wake up, complete disaster. The observers were thrown out of the vote counting centers in every major city where there were still votes left to count. Reports and footage of vans pulling up and unloading at counting centers at 6am. Even worse, our people on the ground are hardly putting up a fuss. After the summer of love and racial harmony no white Republican wants to stand up to an inner-city bureaucrat and end up as the target of the next social media lynch mob. Congratulations, you've just been psyopped. Because physical wounds heal.

The media went into overdrive — FoxNews included — saying that Biden had won the election — even as votes were still being counted days later in Pennsylvania (the State Attorney General decided late ballots counted in defiance of state law), Michigan, and other places. I went to work at Trump HQ taking calls on the voter hotline. It was draining work. First of all, there were a lot of Democrats calling to say some truly demented shit. Things like "We're going to rape every woman in your family and make you watch. Then we'll kill them in front of you. And then we'll rape and kill you too." Most of the volunteers helping take down fraud reports were women ranging from stately older grandmothers to teenage girls. You could tell this sort of thing disturbed them but they soldiered on through the abuse and threats. Rightwing women, God love em. Me, I was quickly coming to the conclusion that it was impossible to live in the same country as libtards and they should all be removed, so to speak. But it wasn't the harassment calls that hit me hard, it was calls like the one I got from the mother of a dead soldier in Georgia who, after getting a piece of mail from the county registrar addressed to her son, checked the state website and found that her son had registered and voted by mail despite having been killed in action several years ago in Afghanistan. I left the phone bank room and went to verify it myself with one of our computer geeks who had access to the voting records. There it was on the computer screen, confirmation he had registered and voted, and in the next browser tab over, his obituary in the local paper. I felt like someone had punched me in the gut.

I continued to work the phones, there were lots of verified reports of stolen ballots from mailboxes, Trump voters showing up at the polls in Pennsylvania only to be told they had already voted early and turned away, machines where the selected candidate was switched when the ballot was printed, a lot of the usual dirty tricks. And then I get a different sort of call. It was from a lady whose neighbor worked for an elections system company and had traveled to one of the crucial battleground states to provide on-site tech support at one of the main counting centers. This lady was out walking with her husband and noticed her neighbor was sitting in a parked car just staring out the windshield. She went over and the neighbor rolled down the window. She welcomed them back and mentioned that they were home from their trip early. They asked "What did you think about the election?" She said that she thought it was terrible and thought the Democrats must have stolen it with ballot harvesting. The neighbor said "It's even worse than that" and began to explain:

"When the count was taken at the end of the night, I had recorded the totals from each machine and matched it to the machine serial number. I was told the machines would be locked up until the final tally was officially recorded by the elections official the next morning so I went back to the hotel for some sleep. Upon return, I discovered that the machines had not actually been locked up. I began checking the totals but they didn't match what they had displayed the night before. The number of votes were the same, but instead showing a strong Trump win as they had at the end of election night, the margin had flipped to a strong Biden win. I reported it to the company and they told me not to breathe a word of it to anyone else and to travel home immediately and wait for further instruction."

I wrote the account down by hand. We had a web based form system that we normally used to record and organize fraud reports with, but we had been getting hit with DDoS attacks all day and I wasn't about to let a witness with a red hot smoking gun get Epsteined. I took it to some trustworthy high-level operatives who moved fast to arrange security for the witness and get this story to the top folks on the campaign.

Back at home, later that night, I'm brushing my teeth and my phone buzzes, I pick up and hear on the other end,

"Hey this is Rudy Giuliani, I'm here with Sidney Powell…" I spit out the toothpaste and stand there for a few seconds having a flashback to the aftermath of 9/11.

From then until January 6th I had held out some hope that the wrong would be righted. But the first mistake of Trump's administration would come back to haunt him as it had so many times during those four years. You're only as strong as the people you surround yourself with, and Trump was surrounded by spineless lizard people, deluded midwits, and outright traitors. He was fond of quoting a poem, The Snake. If only he had took it to heart. As the snake says to the women he bit after she brought him into her house, saving him from the cold, "You knew damn well I was a snake before you took me in." Such goes for the long line of snakes Trump brought into the White House: Henry McMaster, Reince Priebus, Gina Haspel, Mike Kelly, James Mattis, John Bolton, Rex Tillerson, Mike Pompeo, Mark Meadows…the list goes on.

The fundamental problem was this. The most extensive and inclusive voter fraud organization in the history of American politics had just run the op. And it wasn't just run of the mill ballot box stuffing or dead people voting either. Time Magazine ran a story The Secret History of the Shadow Campaign That Saved the 2020 Election where they laid out some of the contours of this vast operation:

"There was a conspiracy unfolding behind the scenes, one that both curtailed the protests and coordinated

the resistance from CEOs. Both surprises were the result of an informal alliance between left-wing activists and business titans... The handshake between business and labor was just one component of a vast, cross-partisan campaign to protect the election—an extraordinary shadow effort dedicated not to winning the vote but to ensuring it would be free and fair, credible and uncorrupted... Their work touched every aspect of the election. They got states to change voting systems and laws and helped secure hundreds of millions in public and private funding. They fended off voter-suppression lawsuits, recruited armies of poll workers and got millions of people to vote by mail for the first time. They successfully pressured social media companies to take a harder line against disinformation and used data-driven strategies to fight viral smears. They executed national public-awareness campaigns that helped Americans understand how the vote count would unfold over days or weeks, preventing Trump's conspiracy theories and false claims of victory from getting more traction. After Election Day, they monitored every pressure point to ensure that Trump could not overturn the result. "The untold story of the election is the thousands of people of both parties who accomplished the triumph of American democracy at its very foundation," says Norm Eisen, a prominent lawyer and former Obama Administration official

*who recruited Republicans and Democrats to the
board of the Voter Protection Program."*

Talk about saying the quiet part out loud. Corporate
power, social media censorship, a wall to wall propaganda
machine (that included FoxNews), an army of lawyers and
crooked judges who illegally suspended election laws, this
thing was a leviathan. And there was another layer too.
The voting machines themselves were compromised. Some
of them were connected to the internet, some of them had
stuxnet type programming buried deep within the machines.
China, Venezuela, and Cuba played an active role in cyber
warfare and hacking. And there was proof. Mil intel had these
guys dead in the water. But Trump's closest advisors acted as
an airlock to prevent him from being briefed on it in time
to mount an effective response. They were either in on it or
burying their heads in the sand, not wanting to come to terms
with the reality that America was in the midst of a communist
revolution. People who tried to get word to Trump of the size
and scale of the fraud had their White House access cut off.
The weeks dragged by. The Supreme Court declined to hear
a case brought by Texas and joined by Alabama, Arkansas,
Florida, Indiana, Kansas, Louisiana, Mississippi, Montana,
Nebraska, North Dakota, Oklahoma, South Carolina, South
Dakota, Tennessee, Utah and West Virginia. All three justices
that Trump nominated voted against taking the case. The
only two who had the guts to say "Yes, we should take a case
that is brought by over a third of the American States" were

Justices Thomas and Alito — Bush judges. Oh the irony. As the January 6th Electoral College vote count drew ever closer, one last constitutional Hail Mary remained. Members of Congress could object to the electors sent by states where the fraud changed the outcome of the state's vote and the vice-president as the presiding officer could reject those slates of electors.

January 6. An enormous crowd of Americans stood on the ellipse in front of the White House. The President was late. Pence had just told him that he would not use his power to reject votes from the states where the fraud occurred. When he finally got up he gave a rambling diatribe. Meanwhile, during the speech Pence had released a letter explaining that he was caving. Folks in the crowd started seeing the news on their phones. Some began to head for the Capitol to protest. Before they could get there, a vanguard of agent provocateurs had already began to smash their way in. By the time most of the regular Trump supporters had arrived, the Capitol Police were welcoming people in as if it was a normal day of visits by tourists. Most of the people behaved as if they were on an unguided tour. Who can forget the photo of the sweet old granny with her little American flag, looking around in awe at the magnificent building?

It was a trap. But one that was only partially successful. Trump posted a video to his social media accounts urging people to "go home in peace". The crowd began to thin and leave. Most of the people who came to DC for the rally had not even been in the vicinity of the Capitol. Most who did treated it as a lark. There was no insurrection. An actual insurrection would have involved heads on pikes and a new revolutionary government established on the spot. The only tragedy that occurred was the murder of Ashli Babbit, an American patriot and veteran who did not endanger anyone. She merely climbed through a window. It was a simulation. But as a simulation it did have enormous power, because it showed that the mechanics of American government are also a simulation. "They have desecrated the Sacred Temple of Democracy" the donkeys brayed. No, the sacred temple was turned into a cheap whorehouse long ago. To desecrate implies that there was something sacred. All modern experience tells us otherwise. Unless your idea of holiness involves bailing out Wall St's reckless gambles with money you extract from the sweat of decent Americans, or approving NIH budgets which are then used to manufacture chimeric bioweapons that kill more of your own people than all foreign wars combined.

It was Trump's admonishment to go home in peace that was the straw that broke the camel's back. Twitter and Facebook took down the video and locked Trump's accounts. That's right, after years of shitposting and threatening to annihilate entire countries, the President of the United States was kicked off the internet for telling people to go home in peace. Why? Because going home peacefully before nightfall was never part of the plan. The FBI had something far more bloody in mind. As night fell on the capitol, the black bloc paramilitary shock troops were to be deployed. The end of the siege would be Carthaginian in its destruction, which would then give license to a broad-spectrum crackdown. As bad as it all was, Trump's last move as President blunted their plans to an extent. So they had to silence him.

This was the moment I knew that the last traces of the ancien regime in America was truly dead and buried. The first step of any successful coup is to seize control of the leader's communications. In a rapid and coordinated succession of announcements, all social media platforms disabled his ability to communicate to the American people. Even Pinterest banned him. It all was shockingly anticlimactic, almost boring in its execution. "This is the way the world ends, not with a bang, but a whimper." - T.S. Eliot

The system can tolerate many things. It can handle months of riots, domestic unrest, murder in the streets, a complete shut down of normal life in the name of social hygiene. But it cannot tolerate being mocked. The federal law enforcement organs that only months earlier bent their knee to domestic terrorists finally leapt into action. Someone had dared to confront the rulers in a way that was a threat — by exposing their weakness and absurdity. Their power is derived solely from the rest of us behaving as if they have it. If all non-politicians just decided that these people no longer mattered they would disappear overnight. The image of panicked congressmen and congresswomen hiding under desks, clutching each other in terror that the people they betrayed might be there to carry out their just vengeance, this shattered the illusion. The response to this was to be overwhelming, to rebuild the dreamworld in which you are supposed to care about what these people think and do. And the Feds didn't have to do this alone, a vast sea of snitches rose up to rat out anyone they saw there. Daughters reported their mothers, fathers reported sons, brothers turned in each other. It is not normal to choose an abstract political concept over your own flesh and blood. At least in Soviet Union the snitches usually did so for some personal or material gain. In America they do it for social media clout.

Much of the continued hysteria over the self-guided Capitol tours is motivated by sheer jealousy. Libtards love protest culture, Pink pussy hats. Madonna baring her innermost desire to bomb the White House to a crowd of hysterical female incels. Occupying the Sacred Temple of Democracy during the Kavanaugh hearings and threatening Senators in the corridors. Burning down Wendy's just because. Looting Target. Smashing up small businesses that will never pay out. Four years of constant protest, all of it fake and gay. And then Trump's supporters show up and put on a visual spectacle of epic proportions. It was cool and edgy and fresh. Whereas lib protests are all derivative of earlier protests — an interrupted pattern of the same tired slogans and tactics that stretch all the way back to the 60s — here was something new and exciting, and the libs continue to whine and complain about it because they will never do anything half as cool.

The book you are about to read chronicles the first 100 days of the new regime, laying bare the absurdity and insanity the way it deserves: through a vital mix of scorn, mockery, and moral gravity. I trust that you will enjoy it much as I have, and take to heart it's central theme: that we are now living under a much different and dystopian system than before, and we must act accordingly. As I write this, over half a year since Jan. 6th, political prisoners continue to be tortured in the DC Lubyanka. Our system is not unlike that of the Soviet Union. As a friend of mine observed, "America spent 50 years fighting the Soviet Union just to become a gay and retarded version of it." Take to heart the hard-learned lessons of the dissidents who went through that hell:

> *"And how we burned in the camps later, thinking: What would things have been like if every Security operative, when he went out at night to make an arrest, had been uncertain whether he would return alive and had to say good-bye to his family? Or if, during periods of mass arrests, as for example in Leningrad, when they arrested a quarter of the entire city, people had not simply sat there in their lairs, paling with terror at every bang of the downstairs door and at every step on the staircase, but had understood they had nothing left to lose and had boldly set up in the downstairs hall an ambush of half a dozen people with axes, hammers, pokers, or whatever else was at hand?... The Organs would very quickly have suffered a shortage of officers and transport and, notwithstanding all of Stalin's thirst,*

*the cursed machine would have ground to a halt! If...
if... We didn't love freedom enough. And even more
– we had no awareness of the real situation.... We
purely and simply deserved everything that happened
afterward."* — Aleksandr Solzhenitsyn, *The Gulag
Archipelago.*

You must love freedom enough, and you must
make yourself aware of the real situation. Use this
book as a starting point, it will help you begin to
grasp the nature of the leviathan we now face.

— Ben Braddock

INTRODUCTION

"When fascism comes to America, it will call itself anti-fascism."

— *Huey Long (attributed)*

For all intents and purposes, on January 6, 2021, America, as founded, ceased to exist. Having been mortally wounded on Election Day, it was smothered with a My Pillow, its remains cremated at noon on January 20th, 2021.

That it happened even now strains credulity. At 9 p.m. Eastern Time on Tuesday, November 3, 2020, by all indications President Donald Trump was well on his way to re-election. Moreover, it would be as close to a landslide victory as the country had seen since 1984, and Ronald Reagan's 49-state wipeout of Walter Mondale. Indeed, despite the China virus lockdown, the constant verbal and often physical beat-downs from Democrat politicians and media (but I repeat myself), and their street thugs in Black Lives Matter and Antifa in the run-up to Election Day, Trump supporters had eagerly attended mass rallies in the tens of thousands across the nation, up to five times a week, week after week. Meanwhile, Joe Biden was mostly kept chained to the radiator in his Delaware basement for weeks on end, dragged out only occasionally for a few carefully staged media events. For a presidential candidate to not be actively on the campaign trail, pandemic or not, was beyond bizarre; it was unheard of. More than that, it was shameful. For whatever reason, the Democrat Party chose this pathetic, sick man to be their standard-bearer. Joe Biden, an angry, ailing, aged, old guard left-wing bull, frustrated and embittered by a failing mental capacity, stung by serious corruption allegations, on top of a couple of spectacularly disastrous past presidential runs as the highlight of a nearly 50-year career of being wrong on every major foreign and domestic policy issue,[1] was seemingly on his way to an ignominious political, and perhaps actual oblivion.

But then a mysterious water main break somewhere in Atlanta (for which no records of work orders for repair can be found)[2] caused officials to stop the count not only there, but for some reason in several other states until the following morning. At midnight, Trump led Biden in Georgia by 356,945 votes, in Michigan by 293,052, in Wisconsin by 112,022 and in Pennsylvania by a whopping 555,189. Yet somehow, by the following morning – after Republican election observers had been forcibly ejected from vote counting centers, windows and doors sealed from prying eyes and pallets of heretofore uncounted ballots trucked in – the situation miraculously had reversed itself. By December 7, after all the recounts, Biden was now up in Georgia by

---

1 https://www.discoverthenetworks.org/organizations/bidens-senate-voting-record-policy-positions

2 https://gellerreport.com/2020/11/when-georgia-halted-counting-open-records-request-finds-no-invoices-or-work-orders-reported-on-election-day-water-main-break-in-atlanta-highly-exaggerated-slow-leak-we-contained-it-quickly.html/

11,779, Michigan 154,188, Wisconsin 20,682 and Pennsylvania by 81,660.[3]

"I'm not saying it was aliens, but…»[4] it is my firm belief that the 2020 election was indeed stolen. Starting as far back as the spring and early summer of that accursed year, the Chinese COVID-19 lockdown – which was supposed to last no more than the first two weeks of March, yet continued well into the following year – was used as a pretext to further degrade already lax election security and institute mail-in ballots nationwide; this, for an election that was to take place eight months later. Even former President Jimmy Carter warned mail-in balloting was rife with fraud – but that was back in 2005, when even a liberal Democrat could sometimes speak the truth.

Commentator Dennis Prager does not come out and declare theft, but he does note some glaring anomalies:[5]

In 132 years, no president has received more votes in his run for reelection and lost. Yet Donald Trump received 10 million more votes in 2020 than in 2016 – and lost.

Trump won 18 of the 19 counties both Democrats and Republicans regard as the "bell-

---

3 https://navarroreport.com

4 https://knowyourmeme.com/memes/ancient-aliens

5 https://www.frontpagemag.com/fpm/2021/01/most-important-question-about-2020-election-dennis-prager/

wether" counties that virtually always go with the outcome of presidential elections. Yet he lost.

He won four bellwether states – Florida, Ohio, Iowa and North Carolina. Yet he lost.

Republicans held onto all the House seats they were defending and gained another 13 seats. Yet, Trump lost.

Add the following to the anomalies:

Unprecedented efforts were made in some states to change election laws.

Mostly Democratic states sent out tens of millions of ballots or applications for absentee ballots to people who never requested them.

Voting began in some states six weeks before Election Day.

People have submitted sworn affidavits at great personal cost and with possible perjury charges that they witnessed ballot tampering on election night.

In this author's estimation, Peter Navarro in The Navarro Report[6] lays out the most detailed case as to how the 2020 election was stolen. That the Democrat Party, along with, for lack of a better word, its co-conspirators in the GOP establishment (especially the governors and state legislatures of the six contested states), the courts up to and including the Supreme Court and the Big Tech social media and internet oligarchy/oligopoly denied President Trump and his legal team both their day in court as well as a voice to present their case to the American people in the court of public opinion merely underscores their collective guilt in the crime.

At the same time, these co-conspirators began a concerted, massive propaganda campaign to brand anyone and everyone who questioned the legitimacy of the election as conspiracy theorists and worse, insurrectionists and traitors. Never mind that these are the same people who only four years earlier did everything they could to declare Trump's victory illegitimate, and formed a "resistance"[7] and instituted "insurance policies"[8] to sabotage his agenda and seek to remove him from office. Much as the Left enjoys shrieking, "dissent is the highest form of patriotism," it evidently only applies when they're the ones doing the dissenting.

On January 6, 2021, things finally came to a head, when thousands of Trump supporters descended on the Capitol in Washington for a massive "Stop the Steal Rally." A group of

6 https://peternavarro.com/the-navarro-report/

7 https://www.washingtontimes.com/news/2020/nov/15/how-democrats-tried-handcuff-donald-trump-start/

8 https://www.americanthinker.com/blog/2018/10/now_we_known_what_strzok_meant_in_that_insurance_policy_text_to_page.html

speakers, including President Trump himself, made one final appeal to Congress to vote "no" on certifying the Electoral College results.

What the vast majority of peaceful rally-goers did not know was that a number of miscreants, since positively identified as members/supporters of Black Lives Matter[9] and Antifa, but disguised in MAGA hats and other pro-Trump attire, either broke into the Capitol building or were actually led in by D.C. Police officers.[10] Unfortunately, a number of actual Trump supporting rally-goers were caught up in the heat of the moment and followed the leaders inside.

Although there followed some minor property damage, the scene was more like a 1950s-era college panty raid than what the media depicted as akin to a latter day storming of the Bastille. Tragically, three people died, evidently of natural causes. But a fourth, a woman named Ashli Babbitt[11,] a 34-year-old Air Force veteran, was shot in the back and killed by a Capitol Police officer, despite the fact that she was unarmed and according to eyewitness accounts was not acting in a violent or threatening manner.

For sure, the Capitol did not burn that day the way D.C. burned six months earlier in the wake of the death of George Floyd when BLM terrorists attempted to scale the White House fence and wound up torching the nearby historic St. John's Church. The Dresdenization of a dozen or so American

9 https://townhall.com/tipsheet/katiepavlich/2021/01/14/blm-activist-arrested-for-after-attuning-capitol-riots-n2583176

10 https://thenationalpulse.com/news/inconsistent-conflicting-and-ignored-threat-assessments-ahead-of-jan-6-capitol-attack/

11 https://redstate.com/streiff/2021/01/07/305949-n305949

cities all through the summer and into the fall was not only ignored by the Left, or dismissed as "mostly peaceful," but the more intellectually honest among them justified, egged on and cheered the violence. When President Trump tried to convince Oregon's leftist governor Kate Brown to call in the National Guard and protect Portland, he was rebuffed time and again.[12]

No matter. Despite the fact that the timing of his speech did not coincide with the actual break in, the content of his speech in no way, shape or form advocated or condoned violence of any kind, and as soon as he learned of what had happened, the President told rally goers to return home quietly and peacefully, the narrative cast Trump as responsible for inciting violent insurrection.

The political process went forward late that night with the final certification of the Electoral College vote in favor of Joe Biden and the fate of the nation was sealed.

And with every major media outlet trumpeting horrifying reports of the attempted "coup" by the President and his supporters, the Democrats got their Reichstag Fire.

The second impeachment trial that soon followed was even more ludicrous than the first, considering the sole purpose of impeachment is to remove a sitting elected official from office, and Trump had been a private citizen since noon on January 20th, 2021. Despite his acquittal in that farce,

---

12 https://nypost.com/2020/08/30/trump-slams-portlands-mayor-calls-for-national-guard-help/

it's hardly a laughing matter.[13] The implications are deadly serious, not just for Trump, his family and his allies, but for anyone who supports him and anyone who stands in the way of Leftist "fundamental transformation."

As Trump himself has said, "In reality, they're not after me, they're after you. I'm just in the way."

With Trump effectively put out of the way, the purges commenced.[14]

> *While official Washington fixates on the plight of an anti-Putin Russian political dissident,[15] American supporters of Donald Trump are being rounded up, imprisoned, transported to the nation's capital, and likely bankrupted over relatively minor crimes to stoke the narrative that an "insurrection" occurred last month.*
>
> *More than 200 people have been charged so far; the FBI has described its effort as a "24/7 full bore extensive operation" and warned that agents from its 56 field offices will be fully engaged.*
>
> *"The scope and scale of these investigations . . . is really unprecedented not only in FBI history but*

---

13 https://www.theepochtimes.com/trump-acquitted-in-second-impeachment-trial_3695836.html

14 https://amgreatness.com/2021/02/04/americas-political-prisoners-first/

15 https://thefederalist.com/2021/02/02/putin-dissident-alexey-navalny-given-fresh-sentence-in-moscow/

in DOJ history," acting Attorney General Michael Sherwin said during a press conference on January 12.

Since all cases will be adjudicated in Washington, D.C., it's a sure bet that defendants will be shown no mercy in the Trump-hating Beltway legal system also responsible for prosecuting Roger Stone and Lt. Gen. Michael Flynn – just a few of the Americans targeted by law enforcement solely based on their ties to Donald Trump.

Authorities admit that the Justice Department's various sedition strike forces will leverage minor offenses in an attempt to manufacture bigger cases against Trump allies. "Some of the misdemeanors we're filing, these are only the beginning, this is not the end," Sherwin warned. "We're looking at significant felony cases tied to sedition and conspiracy. Their only marching orders from me are to build sedition and conspiracy charges related to the most heinous acts that occurred in the Capitol, and these are significant charges that have felonies with prison terms of up to 20 years..."

...it stands in stark contrast to the way the same law enforcement authorities handled Black Lives Matter rioters in Washington, D.C. last year –prosecutors dropped nearly all charges against hundreds of rioters for more severe crimes including destruction

*of property and assaulting police officers. That sort
of selective treatment played out in cities across the
country, and still does.*

*One set of Americans, based on their political alle-
giance, not only escape punishment but are heralded
as heroes of democracy. The other group is demonized
as traitors, harassed by the news media, denied bail
for minor offenses and presumed guilty until proven
innocent before partisan judges and prosecutors.*

It's frightening enough that our federal law enforcement
and national security apparatus sabotaged first the candidacy
and then the entire presidential term of Donald Trump in
their initial, non-stop attempt to oust him before 2021.
But now, elements of our private sector are working hand-
in-hand to identify and persecute citizens whose actions or
political views do not toe the party line.[16]

*It turns out that the Fourth Amendment is as easily
ignored as the First Amendment... if you get corporations to do the jobs the Constitution forbids to the
government.*

*Once upon a time, only the government was powerful
enough to censor people, and it was only the state that
had the criminal laws and police power that made*

---

16 https://www.americanthinker.com/blog/2021/02/bank_of_america_is_working_with_
the_fbi_to_hunt_down_trump_supporters.html

illegal searches an issue. Now, though, corporations have taken over the public squares in which speech once took place, and they possess every bit of private information we own.

Because the corporations and the federal government share common values (after all, they all went to the same colleges and were taught the same way of thinking), they are tag-teaming: the Democrat-run bureaucracy, White House, and Congress express an unconstitutional desire, and the corporations fill it without implicating that hoary old document...

...It turns out that Bank of America voluntarily got on the computer and searched its databases – that means that it searched your private financial records – to learn whether you traveled to D.C., stayed anywhere within a vast radius of D.C., bought anything at a weapons store in D.C. (whether ammo or a can opener), and bought airline tickets to anywhere.

Stalin's head of the secret police, Lavrentiy Beria, once said, "Show me the man, and I'll show you the crime." Biden's new government/bank fusion says, "Show me the bank records of a visit to D.C., and I'll show you a radical white supremacist insurrectionist who needs to be dragged in for questioning." After all, that's what happened to this man.

*If you're not terrified right now — whether or not you were anywhere near D.C. — you're not reading the situation right. —**What we're witnessing is the federal government's police power and the corporate world's information power coming together to perform a complete end-run around the United States Constitution.***

Emphasis mine. As preternaturally invasive and freedom-killing as our current "progressive" government and its bureaucracies have become since the New Deal, what pundit Andrea Widburg accurately describes is the birth of a tyranny that is orders of magnitude more thoroughly all-encompassing, powerful and malignant as to make even the most repressive regimes on earth seem like comparative pushovers. Certainly, corrupted law enforcement agencies will be a part of the apparatus of coercion, but as evidenced by the actions of Bank of America in this instance, will play only a supporting role.

Forget the phony Reichstag Fire of January 6, 2021. The information that millions of us blindly coughed up not just on social(ist) media but everywhere over the past 25 to 30 years since the burgeoning of the digital age has not only been monetized by the neo-maxi-zoom-dweebies[17] of the Billionaire Soys Club like Mark Zuckerberg and Jack Dorsey, but is primed and ready to be used as the ultimate tool of coercion and submission. If, or perhaps when, we abolish

---

17 https://www.urbandictionary.com/define.php?term=Neo-Maxi%20Zoomdweebie

cash and institute digital currency, anything and everything you purchase will be compiled, indexed, filed, numbered, referenced and cross-referenced for anything "troubling." Not just cigarettes, booze, a 32-ounce soda or even porn, but firearms, ammo, an American flag, $500 worth of State of Israel Bonds, a contribution to the Police Benevolent Association, a subscription to the Epoch Times and so on. And when you want to buy a house, a car or health insurance (assuming private health insurance is not outlawed), you might get a little note from some government apparatchik stating you have to turn over all your weapons since "owning firearms is dangerous to your health."

This is what happens when two to three generations of our children are brainwashed all day every day from kindergarten through post-graduate. You don't need a Secret Police when potentially anyone including your own family members will do that job for free in order to "stop white supremacy" or "save the planet" or "save our democracy."»[18]

> *Therese Duke told the Boston Herald she was innocently "looking for a place to eat" in Washington, D.C., with "like-minded" Trump supporters when they were accosted by counter-protesters near the White House.*

---

18 https://nypost.com/2021/01/17/therese-duke-massachusetts-mom-punched-at-dc-rally-loses-job/

The melee on Jan. 5 – the night before rioters stormed the Capitol – saw her getting punched in the face, with her sister getting arrested for retaliating against the alleged attacker.

"I did nothing wrong," Duke insisted to the Herald. "I was the one who was assaulted."

She soon went viral, however, when her 18-year-old daughter, Helena Duke, mocked her as she identified her as being the woman in a video now seen more than 12 million times.

"Hi mom remember the time you told me I shouldn't go to BLM protests because they could get violent... this you?" her daughter asked.

The nurse said that since then, she has been "getting threats" and UMass Memorial Health Care confirmed online that she is "no longer a part of our organization."

Duke said she felt "forced" to resign from her job of 15 years, although the Herald noted that in an online fundraiser, she had admitted she had been "relieved from my employment pending an investigation." She now fears her notoriety will crush her chances of finding new work. "Anybody can Google me," she told the Herald. "Nobody will hire me."

* * * * *

One hundred days is recognized as a benchmark in American politics by which a new presidential administration is measured. It's considered the window of opportunity to push its agenda forward, seemingly with the political winds at its back. Of course, this is only the case when a Democrat controls the White House as, per the media, he'll always have a popular mandate (even when he doesn't) to enact the most radical and transformative of politically toxic legislation no matter how slim his margin of victory – or if he even won the election in the first place. During this roughly 14-week period, the Biden junta inflicted or began pushing hard to inflict on us the following:

- An intentional migrant "crisis" that effectively erases our southern border and is a gateway for amnesty for tens of millions of illegal aliens.

- Trillions more added to the debt and deficits via Chinese COVID relief and infrastructure boondoggles.

- Statehood for D.C. and Puerto Rico.

- Court packing.

- Abolition of the Electoral College.

- Abandonment of the filibuster in the Senate.

- "Green New Deal" madness that will destroy the petrochemical industry and build a mass grave back to the 12th century.

- H.R. 1 "For the People Act" that institutionalizes election rigging on behalf of Democrats, giving them permanent electoral power.

- Alienating our allies and knuckling under to our enemies abroad, specifically China, Iran and Russia.

- Reparations for blacks.

- Dismantling of the U.S. military, declaring "climate change" and "white nationalism" our top national security threats while indoctrinating the ranks with anti-American propaganda, including Critical Race Theory

Over 40 executive orders within the first 100 days alone that are so massive, damaging and virtually irreversible that they give FDR's disastrous New Deal a run for the money (literally).[19]

Aside from this official/traditional presidential honeymoon period, another, much more significant one hundred-day period began two months before the installation of Joe Biden. It was bookended by the theft of the 2020 Presidential election and then the second attempt to impeach Donald Trump solely for the purpose of preventing his being

19 https://www.youtube.com/watch?v=q_r_XahzELY

able to run in 2024. Even more ominously, 100 days after the election saw the Defense Department's Stalinist purge of the US military of what it deemed "extremists" in the ranks; that is, anyone in uniform who is white, Christian, conservative, questioned the outcome of the election, and opposed the transformation of the armed forces into a social justice experiment and the dismantling of America as founded, or what's left of it.

This book is a serialization/compilation of my *Morning Report* columns at *Cut Jib Newsletter*[20] and *Ace of Spades HQ*,[21] for the 100 days between November 3, 2020 and February 10, 2021. These daily posts consist of an aggregation of links to the day's top stories as well as an editorial built around one or two of the lead items. In reviewing them for this book, I had to revisit the multiple outrages of what Rush Limbaugh used to call "the daily soap opera." And I got angry all over again.

More than ever, those 100 days have made it clear that the media is either a propaganda arm pushing the Marxist agenda or, as some have postulated, the actual source of the agenda itself, with the Democrat Party its instrument of implementation. It is collectively they, after all, who control the narrative and the news cycles; and who, when the oftentimes multiple outrages du jour have passed their prime, move seamlessly on to the next one, day in and day

---

20 cutjibnewsletter.com

21 ace.mu.nu

out. Between the constant attacks on President Trump, the Chinese coronavirus lockdowns, the wave of urban terrorism unleashed in the wake of George Floyd's death, two separate shampeachments; then the climax of the stolen election and the staged January 6 Capitol Hill "riot," it's all too easy to become numb to it all, all but forgetting the incidents and players that gave you agita in the first place.

But we cannot let them get away with flushing them down the memory hole. Our outrage is something none of us should want to lose, not merely for the value in the power of that emotion, but to be able to back it up with the hard cold facts that caused it.

In writing my blogposts, I begin aggregating links for news stories the night before, from upwards of 20 news and opinion sites, and early the next morning, after adding some final links from sites that refresh early or anything breaking. Then, I set about writing an editorial based on the leading story of the day, and hit "publish" no later than 7:30 a.m.

My style is (hopefully) delivered with wit, humor and sometimes a soupçon of schtick. Because it's early and I'm racing against the clock to publish, as I write I'm forced to go with my first instincts and to keep the editing to a bare minimum, with grammar, punctuation and redundancy being casualties of speed. Yet it's precisely the immediacy and rawness of emotion as I react to the outrages *du jour* that reflect the way the site's readers and commenters are reacting, thinking and feeling.

I wanted to keep that immediacy in this book – the visceral sense of what it felt like living through this terrifying history – so aside from clarifying some of the more colorful nicknames and phrases that regular readers know (see the footnotes), the essence of each day's entry, edited down to fit the constraints of this format, is as it was published. Taken as a whole, it represents a diary and day-by-day chronicle of one of the most pivotal chapters - and perhaps the final one – in American history.

These 100 Days, the days that followed and the ones yet to come long after this book will have been published will bring outrages and tragedies as bad and no doubt even worse than those reported and remarked on here. It is my belief, though, that ultimately, our decency, humanity and whatever vestiges of the American spirit that still live in each of us can overcome this disaster. How that manifests itself - if it manifests itself - has yet to unfold. But considering the state of this nation and, indeed, the world at the time of this writing, whether I or someone else will be allowed to chronicle those days is still very much in doubt.

100 DAYS

"And so it begins."

— The Guy That Always Says "And So It Begins"

Tuesday, November 3, 2020

There is an apocryphal quote attributed to a witness of the execution of Charles I. As the axe fell he reportedly said, "that so good a man should be so bad a king." Disregarding the circumstances surrounding the utterance of that phrase, in terms of Trump, perhaps it's appropriate to say "that so flawed a man should be so outstanding a president." But having said that, what really are this man's "flaws?" In the cold light of day, they are petty and meaningless. "Make America Great Again" is not just a catchy phrase or a campaign slogan. For Trump, it is a mantra and a way of life. Whatever he has achieved in his life because of his education, skills, drive and support from his family could not have happened anywhere else. It was the greatness of America, the freedom to succeed or fail and start over on one's own terms that made him great. One of the rhetorical kill-shots of the final debate (not quite two weeks but which seems like it was ages ago) was when Trump said...

"You know, Joe, I ran because of you. I ran because of Barack Obama, because you did a poor job. If I thought you did a good job, I would've never run. I would've never run. I ran because of you. I'm looking at you now, you're a politician. I ran because of you." [22]

Those words are just pregnant with meaning. More than mere policy, or problem-solving, Trump understood that it was not only what those two, their party as well as the GOP-e collaborators didn't accomplish in eight years, but what they were complicit in for years and even decades before Donald J. Trump even entertained the possibility of running for office: the methodical dismantling of the very things, stated above, that made not only the success of Donald Trump but every other hard-working, G-d-fearing, law-abiding American possible. Look at what he, his family, friends and his loyal team have been put through since he came down the escalator at Trump Tower five-and-a-half years ago. To say it's been a living hell is an understatement.

Look at what we who supported him have been put through: everything from cement hate-shakes, bike locks, beat downs, blood-libeling, bullets and arson, to censorship, ridicule, intimidation and loss of employment for daring to exercise our rights to express our opinion guaranteed in a sacred document; one which those who abuse us seek to destroy while conveniently hiding behind its very protections when called out.

---

22 https://www.breitbart.com/politics/2020/10/22/trump-joe-biden-i-ran-because-you/

No, Donald J. Trump did not need to do this. Donald J. Trump felt he HAD to do this.

The final sentence before the signatures on The Declaration of Independence reads:

And for the support of this Declaration, with a firm reliance on the protection of divine Providence, we mutually pledge to each other our Lives, our Fortunes and our sacred Honor.[23]

The 56 men who signed that document on July 4th, 1776 knew full well that had they not gained independence for the colonies, they were signing their own death warrant. Even if, please G-d, President Trump wins reelection, when he leaves office at noon on January 20th, 2025 he, his children and his grandchildren will be targeted for retribution for all time by the forces who, until he came along, were well on the way to "fundamentally transforming" America into a vassal state of surpassing mediocrity and misery to be lorded over by puppets of a global government, itself controlled by the Chi-Coms.

To risk all of that, with one's eyes wide open, truly takes an individual with character, faith in the Almighty and when you get right down to it, guts. I cannot even put into words how I personally feel about being proud for the first time in my adult life to cast a vote for someone. It's up there with the trepidation I feel about who comes after this president.

---

23 https://thelibertyherald.com/2020/07/04/we-mutually-pledge-to-each-other-our-lives-our-fortunes-and-our-sacred-honor/

Trump cannot be a one-off. He must not be a one-off. The enthusiasm and energy of tens of thousands of people at those rallies just can't be for one man; it has to be for a movement that heralds a national revival.

Yes, we owe a debt of gratitude to President Donald Trump that can never be repaid — except of course to go out and cast a vote for this man.

Wednesday, November 4, 2020

I'm sick to my friggin' stomach. As of right now while the election is in suspended animation as we wait on Milwaukee and Philadelphia to manufacture enough phony votes to steal the national election, or at least attempt to steal it, Trump is hanging onto the lead in Pennsylvania (+640,000), Georgia (+100,000), North Carolina (+100,000) and Michigan (+200,000). He's down in Wisconsin (-14,000), Arizona (-93,000) and Nevada (-7,500).

For the past G-d knows how many months I have been stating that despite the lockdowns and intentional tanking of the economy, as well as the mail-in ballot madness, Trump was going to win re-election clearly if not decisively *the cheat factor notwithstanding.* Of course, Democrat hinky meshugas and even voter intimidation a la the New Black Panthers circa 2008 was to be expected. But in a sane world, given who this President is and what he has achieved against his rival as well as all the other things like enthusiasm, there was just no way in hell the Democrat Industrial Propaganda Complex could pull off a cheat to end all cheats.

While Malig-Nancy Pelosi and Hillary the Popeil Collapsible Wonder Bollard[24] are vile hags, when they flapped their dentures about Biden never conceding was a shot across the bow. And then, with the in-your-face bullshit early on of thug operatives in Philly barring legitimate GOP poll watchers from polling places and openly crowing about it, and then Fox news calling Virginia and Arizona, while waiting ages to call Florida and one or two other states for Trump when he was the clear winner to even Stevie Wonder in a blindfold, and then a pipe suddenly bursting in the office where votes are being tabulated in Fulton County, to Philadelphia putting a lid on vote counting until later today because, reasons! And on and on and on. This Mickey Mouse banana republic garbage is so blatant and in your face that Zombie Papa Doc Duvalier just phoned from hell to say "le dude! I can smell it down here!" While the Florida victory was so fantastically huge and driven by a usually reliable Democrat bloc – Latinos – the fear of socialism is still visceral even in the younger generations who might not have experienced it first hand. That is a positive. But there are a few warning bells about last night should the unthinkable happen:[25]

"That the senile and corrupt Joe Biden could finish so strong speaks to either the gullibility or unserious-

---

24 Hillary Clinton

25 https://www.americanthinker.com/blog/2020/11/election_night_reveals_three_disturbing_facts.html

ness of far too many Americans. Biden obviously has mental acuity issues and has a history of corruption, but that did not seem to be a big deal to the Americans who voted for him. I guess the probability of more lockdowns are lost on a number of Americans who are more frightened by the Wuhan virus than the probability of America becoming a socialist, if not communist, nation under a Biden presidency...

...By sitting on the results of states like Georgia and North Carolina, states that, of this writing, showed Trump with narrow leads with 99 percent of the precincts in, Fox allowed Biden to gain momentum while slowing Trump's dominance. It looks like the influence of RINO Paul Ryan as a Fox Corporation board member and the legacy of analyst Bill Sammon (Fox News VP Politics) resulted in a psy-ops (psychological operations) campaign against conservative morale...

... States like Wisconsin, Michigan and Pennsylvania declaring they need more days to count their votes also raises the specter of voter fraud. Globalists, corrupt voting officials and the deep state are most likely in on this skullduggery. Through this coordinated effort, along with the media, the race is close and the stage is set for either stealing the election for Biden, civil unrest, or both."

Whatever transpires today and in the days that follow, President Trump is not going to lay down and die. I am assuming that his legal teams are on the ground especially in PA to fight the cheat with every legal means at their disposal. And G-d forbid this does go to the SCOTUS, well, the seating of Amy Coney Barrett looms exceedingly large.

Let's face it; Donald Trump did in fact win re-election last night. What we are watching now is just another stage of the coup that started five years ago to destroy him and us.

Thursday, November 5, 2020

Day Two of what I pray is not the descent into Year Zero begins with rage and confusion. The situation on the ground is that the lawsuits are flying while the Democrat Deep State Machine stands on the nearly dead corpse of the republic to proclaim the system works and we should all come together and heel, er, heal. Or some such rot. Most outrageously, those controlling the zombified Joe Biden have a Biden-Harris Transition website already live. If there is a G-d in Heaven, then that kind of arrogance and hubris I pray comes back to haunt them.

As it is, it is taking every ounce of energy I have to fight the sinking feeling that they will get away with this. I should have sensed this was going to happen but even after everything we had been through with this President and before, I really didn't think what they just did was possible. Oh, election meshugas happens and it does affect outcomes here and there, or on a national level in some fluke cases like 1960 or almost in 2000 where sanity (or so we thought at the time) prevailed. But for blatant election tampering and voter intimidation in PA and AZ, the national news media to blatantly call races for Biden that were still active while delaying the calls for major victories for Trump, and then for those five or six crucial states to stop their counting for no legitimate reason at all (a burst water pipe?!), then suddenly "discover" tens of thousands of ballots, with no signatures or even postmarks that are 100% for Biden and ZERO marked for Trump, that is not random. That is a coordinated attack to sabotage the election by the Democrat Deep State Globalists. They knew weeks ago that Trump was going to at a minimum have a clear win of the Electoral College and perhaps even a narrow margin of the popular vote if not a landslide. The pollsters didn't "get it wrong." They were spewing propaganda as part of a psychological warfare operation to depress Trump voters. As if the tens of thousands of rally attendees going bonkers for Trump would believe it.

Look, Malig-Nancy Pelosi may be a classless, corrupt daughter of a mobster who's only marginally more articulate than Goofy Joey Biden. But back in July, she had this to say about President Trump:

> *"The fact is: Whether he knows it yet or not,*
> *he will be leaving."*

She didn't say, "I'm confident he will be defeated," or "Joe Biden is beating him badly in the polls so there's no way he can win," or something like that. The words she used were a tell. Yes, you can argue that she suffers Trump Derangement Syndrome, but I think that it was her TDS that got the better of her and she tipped her hand as to what was up. What I'm driving at is that everything I cited above proves that what happened on Tuesday was a coordinated, multi-pronged, pre-planned event. Pelosi's words just underscore it.

Traitorous, treasonous vermin like Stanley McChrystal are expert at staging so-called "color revolutions" that may resemble grassroots uprisings of "the people" against "tyrants." He is part of the Deep State Globalist cabal and I would not be surprised if the election thievery, along with the threatened violence of the Antifa/BLM street thugs who will be portrayed by the Industrial Agitprop Media disinformation complex as "ordinary citizens fighting for their freedom" as well as the former's election night disinformation op are all interconnected. From everything I have seen over the past four years, you can bet your bottom social credit score credit on it.

So, what can we do? We have a column from Spengler (David Goldman) assuring us that with the Senate still in GOP hands and perhaps a razor thin margin either way in a divided House, as well as a 5-4 or even 6-3 SCOTUS because of ACB, a Joe-Kamal administration will be completely hand-cuffed for four years.[26] With all do respect to Spengler, these

---

26 https://pjmedia.com/spengler/2020/11/04/the-good-news-is-that-biden-is-screwed-even-if-he-wins-n1124975

fucking criminals just did the unthinkable and actually stole a national election after spending four years doing the other unthinkable and attempt to illegally reverse the previous election. Do you really think they are going to be bothered by the niceties of the Constitution, regular order, tradition and – wait for it – ethics?!

We also have Miranda Devine insisting "the Dems will not get away with this"[27] as well as the outstanding Michael Anton stating "It will all go according to plan — unless we stop it."[28] Well, Mr. Anton I am open to suggestions. To my mind, the only way to do that requires the five or six armored or airborne divisions to seize the statehouses and legislatures in question, arrest every damned Democrat in sight, seize all the ballots and/or thumbdrives (evidently that's a thing in Michigan) and declare Donald J. Trump as the winner based on the real projections at about the time on Tuesday night when the Chinese yuan crashed.

And since that is probably not going to happen except in my mind, I don't know really what can be done. The whole thing is now a hot mess of phony ballots, real ballots and the rules and regulations of six states, some of them changed literally almost at the last second before election day to make it impossible to reject clearly bogus ballots. How are the courts or Supreme Court going to clear that up, assuming we have a majority that wants to do so?

---

27 https://nypost.com/2020/11/04/biden-may-steal-an-election-for-the-elitists-but-dems-will-regret-it-devine/

28 https://amgreatness.com/2020/11/04/game-on-for-the-coup/#comment-77640

Look, for better or worse, in elections past when things did not go the way I wanted, I swallowed, bit the bullet and then moved on. But I never thought in a billion billion years that the American system of free and fair elections would ever be anything but that. And here we are, on par with Zimbabwe in 1980, or Mexico for nearly 100 years with the PRI (which is indeed where we are headed). Yes, the average Democrat voter is upset about what happened NOT because their party sabotaged the election but that they did not get the clear victory they were promised. And now, if Trump does in fact survive this not-so-soft coup attempt, it will further tear the country apart. Not that there is any love lost between the Left and America as founded (or what vestige is left of it). Funny how if Trump does win the shrieking about how the Constitution was ignored or destroyed will be deafening. Ironic, and disgusting at the same time.

It's one thing when the thug terrorists of Antifa/BLM say "by any means necessary." It's quite another when what is supposed to be one of the two major American political parties says it as well and takes it to heart. They lost this election. They know they lost this election. Worse for them, they have lost a good chunk of their base – the disaffected, disenfranchised and so-called "marginalized" "victims" ironically enough who are that way because of Democrat policies. The Deep State machinations of power, thievery and perversion wrapped in privilege also took a massive hit insofar as it was exposed to the people. They lost this election months ago if not a year ago before the phony pandemic hit. They lost it when Trump stated to their faces and for the whole world to see on January 20th, 2017 when he promised to drain the swamp.

But the swamp is wide and it is deep, as we have now seen. So I ask Ms. Devine and Messrs. Goldman and Anton, who are no doubt sincere in their words, yes let's fight back and not let this happen.

The question is "HOW?"

Friday, November 6, 2020

We're barely hanging on by the flagellum of an albino bacteria. On a positive note, the court in Pennsylvania ordered ballot counting to be halted with questionable ballots to be set aside, and I believe there is also some hopeful signs out of Nevada and Arizona. But now I see Alaska is in the middle of this garbage? WTAF?! That said, in all honesty, I do not know what combinations of which states Trump must win in order to get to 270 electoral votes, but at this point I don't really care. No, I do care, it's just that there's a bigger picture to focus on than the tactics and machinations of a process that is so obviously corrupted; not just at the level of the thugs dumping phony ballots in the middle of the night or barring the counting process of duly certified observers, but the legal system and judges that are rubber stamping the fraud.

And that goes directly to the heart of the problem. We witnessed in real time on Tuesday night and over the ensuing two days the actual theft of a national election. Let me add the word "attempted" because for now, they've been caught in the act, but the situation is still in doubt, at least in terms of the normal, legal, procedural channels for attempting to rectify this situation. First of all, I do NOT trust the Supreme Court of the United States to redress this because I do not trust Roberts. Even so, what is there to judge as of this moment? As much as 2000 was a fiasco, no matter what happened George W. Bush was going to legally win that election and be president. On Tuesday the sabotage happened while things were in progress, so SCOTUS (unless I am wrong) cannot pick a winner based on things as they stand. Hence the rush to "count every vote!" Including forgeries, fakes and dead people.

So from my understanding, option one is a recount process that allows every single questionable ballot to be tossed. But what constitutes questionable, considering Roberts (piss be upon him) allowed Pennsylvania to accept ones with no signature or postmarked after November 3rd, and who gets to decide it anyway? Option two is to call for another vote in each state where the count is muddled. Although there is precedent the Democrats will scream bloody murder. Hell they and the media are already sliming Trump as a sore loser and that there was no fraud at all. In any case, the same thugs and crooks are the ones who will monitor those elections (although I assume Team Trump will not allow that if it gets to that point).

The only other thing I see is the states that have GOP-controlled legislatures can exercise their Constitutional authority under Article II to appoint the electors of their choosing to the Electoral College, based on the fact that the elections in their state are provably corrupted or otherwise inconclusive. I ain't no Mark Levin but I believe this situation qualifies. Their governors, attorneys general and secretaries of state have no power to stop them. IIRC the only other time this was done was 1824 (cue Tommy Vietor) but G-d bless the framers, they put this in there for just such an emergency. But, given a host of obvious political reasons, what are the odds that this happens?

If I'm missing something else, please comment. I'm punchy and exhausted over this but I didn't necessarily want to focus on this aspect anyway. President Trump is figuratively and no doubt literally fighting for his life and that if his family, allies and associates. He is going to exhaust every legal means at his disposal to stop what would be the first-degree murder of the United States of America. It would be nice, don't you think, if every elected official in the Republican Party stood shoulder to shoulder with him. Yet almost as revolting as the spectacle we are enduring has been the almost complete abandonment of Trump by his own party. I don't give a shit about the judicial appointments and the three SCOTUS justices; for Mitch McConnell yesterday to come out and state that he is willing to work with a President Biden to appoint "moderates" or some such rot is really the bitter end. And why the hell is Ron Johnson not on the ground in Madison? David Perdue in Atlanta? Or eve Lisa Murkowski up in Juneau?

Hell, why isn't every Republican Senator and Congress-man standing with him at a press conference declaring in unison that this election has been corrupted and must either be redone or Donald Trump declared the winner as he was well on his way to becoming? Sadly, tragically, that is a rhetorical question. I said before the election in at least two pitches that Trump is no doubt one of the greatest presidents in American history, for sure in the top four or five. It's not only because of his remarkable accomplishments, many of which he achieved with at most the grudging support of his own party while he was under constant assault and persecution from the overt and covert attempts to sabotage his first term. President Trump is one of our greatest presidents because he exposed the rot, the criminality, the perversion, the corruption and the hypocrisy of an entrenched group of holier-than-thou thugs who for decades have been sucking the life out of our blessed land and heritage for their own personal or political gain.

Let's not sugarcoat it; it's evil. He exposed it, tried like hell to fight it and even now, he's still in there and is not going to give up. As painful as it is to say this, as far as I'm concerned, America is dead. It's better to face that fact than to keep on deluding ourselves otherwise. Even if by some miracle Trump manages to win just one more time, we still face what is in fact an implacable and formidable enemy in our midst. The Democrat Party, the Deep State bureaucracy, a lying propagandistic media, and the brainwashing mills of academia. And in two years time and then another two we'll have to do this all over again.

It's one thing to have rigged elections in places like Haiti or Iran. When your economy is in ruins and there's no work or food, it's easy for ordinary people to take to the streets and attempt to oust the tyrants. Over here, only one side of that equation is in effect. The illusion of normalcy still exists. Naturally, it's projected by the Democrats as we the majority of decent people looked upon as a minority of violent racists led by an orange-tinged demagogue who's literally Hitler. That said, while we bitch and moan about what our so-called leaders aren't doing, what are we doing? Or better still, given the situation, what can we do? Or G-d forbid what are we willing to do?

Whatever the outcome, the Left and everything in this country that it controls must be defeated and never allowed near the instrumentalities of political and societal control and influence. Forget the Constitution, the rule of law or anything else. Perhaps in a sense, it really is outdated, insofar as evil people have been using it as a cudgel and a shield to conquer us from within. But it's not the failings of that document or the men who drafted it. It's the failings of the citizenry who over time lost their sense of morality and ethics. There is no difference between the goon who refused to let in a legitimate poll watcher in to do his job than there is for Chief Justice John Roberts. Or the mouth-breathing asshole who registered someone who's been dead for 36 years to cast a vote for Biden than there is of Biden himself.

Monday, November 9, 2020

Despite the constant drumbeat from the Democrat Anti-Media Complex as well as the traitors, flunkies and sellouts in the party formerly known as Republican, the fact of the matter remains that Joe Biden is NOT the president-elect. As I would like to remind anyone who thinks that the media's designation of a winner actually means anything, I invite you now to list the top highlights of the Al Gore administration, from either of his two terms in office. If that's too tough, then tell us all about all the great things President Dewey accomplished.

While I let you go off and sharpen your pencil, this week begins the concerted effort by Team Trump to present its evidence, physical as well as in the domain of forensic accounting, to show that in six states where President Trump was well on the way to carrying, the counts were illegally halted, and then pre-marked ballots for Biden were dumped at polling/tabulation sites or blank ballots where armies of accomplices filled them in. All this as legally authorized poll watchers were physically barred from witnessing the crime. And that doesn't even include a computer tabulation program that is used widely across the nation that has been found to accidentally on purpose switch Trump votes to Biden, but oddly, never the other way around. But I digress.

We all know what's at stake if GOD FORBID we the people have an election stolen and Joe "von Hindenburg" Biden is installed. Hell, that's exactly why Trump won more

votes across a broader spectrum of voters including traditional Democrat blocs than every before, and massively. And
that is exactly why what you saw Tuesday night just as the
Chinese Yuan crashed go down the way it did. Oh indeed,
normal early voting plus the inherent and pre-planned fraud
from Mail-In Voting on the pretext of the phony pandemic
panic if those are ever examined will no doubt be filled to
the rim with dead people, illegal aliens, extraterrestrials and
multiples of same. In fact, it's my guess that even the deepest
of deep blue states that are not being contested were probably
a hell of a lot closer than the final results show. Trump got
historic levels of black support in every major metropolitan
area except in Philly, Pittsburgh, Detroit, Milwaukee and
Atlanta. Are black voters that much culturally different from
those in Florida, for example? Maybe in an era before mass-
media there would certainly be regional cultural differences
but not in 2020. Not politically anyway. But I digress yet
again.

So at 9:00PM on Election Night, with Trump ahead
significantly and sweeping through the south and on his
way to sweep across the Midwest and Northern states, the
networks refused to call those he would clearly be projected
to win while the count was stopped for the night and the poll
watchers barred from their duty. Then, voila! Biden goes from
being down by several hundred thousand to being ahead by
a few thousand. Meh, I'm rehashing things we already know
but that Leftists refuse to hear and worse the media will not
allow to be broadcast. And worse, I am getting away from the

point I want to make to kick off today and to prime us for the week or perhaps weeks ahead.

I am a realist about things but I am an optimist. I would follow Donald Trump through the gates of Hell for all he has done for this country. Not just the policy things which in any honest assessment of history were phenomenal but his desire to finally make government accountable and break up the racket that's been rotting this country from the inside since the end of World War 2. For that, he had to be destroyed. And the situation is still hanging in the balance.

While the Left pounded us furiously over the weekend, the President remained essentially silent. His surrogates took to the airwaves to declare this fight far from over while all of us oscillated between wild optimism and the depths of depression. Let's be real: the evil that is arrayed against Trump and us is vast and deep. Despite what we saw unfold since last Tuesday it has to pass a number of very high hurdles because we are talking about a national election, not a parking ticket. And no matter that even the most neophyte student of the Constitution understands that these results are so tainted that they should be tossed, given the depth of corruption of our politicians as well as our judges over the years, I'm troubled to say the least.

But I came to the conclusion yesterday that the President and his team do in fact have not only a case but have the goods to at the very least, get him to at least the bare minimum of Electoral Votes, if not more, to claim the win. More crucially, despite the constant character assassination for well over five years, Donald Trump I believe does have integrity. I do not think that he would drag this thing on and on knowing that it was a lost cause. On a purely mercenary level, it would destroy the Trump name as a brand if you will. But I think it goes much deeper than that. He would lose not just the election, but he would have utterly crushed the spirit of millions of people to not only not ever trust anyone ever again but to give up on America. And then it really would be lights out for a very long time.

No, this man knows he has a case and he is going to fight all the way to the very end for vindication and justice. And that is why while given all the forces and factors arrayed against him, despite the evidence, I am not going to give up on him. [29]

"You know how they kept talking about the red mirage? Well, this is the blue smokescreen.

It's not really very convincing, and you can kind of squint through it and see the antifa goons looking all sad-faced, and how the low-info lefties are going to be disappointed like the kiddies who got a healthy snack for Halloween. Honestly, guys, if you look at this the right way, you'll still be hopping mad, but you have to have a heart of steel not to laugh like a hyena.

---

29 https://pjmedia.com/columns/sarah-hoyt/2020/11/08/dont-jump-off-that-ledge-this-is-just-a-blue-smokescreen-n1131834

Things are bad for the Dems. Really bad.

You see, they thought that they had frauded (totally a word) enough in advance, and the polls assured them they were doing fine. Then, come Election Day, that darn Trump pulled off a landslide election, and they had to stoop to counting and do their best to manufacture more votes ASAP...

The right is mad as hell. We have reason to be. And the left is terrified. Or at least those in the know are terrified.

This wasn't the normal, carefully planned, subtle fraud. This was fraud created the same way that one breaks into a bank with two sticks of dynamite, instead of picking at the lock.

Such fraud leaves traces. If we look into it we'll find them. And once we find them, even some secure blue states with all vote-by-mail will be looked at.

And when Trump wins, despite all this nonsense (yes, the left will riot. But that will be different from the last year, how?), and things are looked into, they might lose their permanent fiefdoms created by "all vote-by-mail" states. And then what?...

Years ago, during the '04 election, a friend told me the Democrats always get louder and more triumphalist when they're losing. I've observed this is true, since then.

So, step down from the ledge. Go take a shower. Have some real food. Eat a vegetable. Ease up on the coffee. Go for a walk.

And don't fall for the blue smokescreen. And DO NOT abandon Trump. He's got this, if you guys don't stab him in the back. He's got this all the way. Let him play it.

Yes, the Republic is in danger, and yes, things can still go wrong because a lot of the institutions are corrupted.

But the left is covered in flop sweat. They don't think they're going to win this.

At least they won't if you don't let them into your head."

Take heart and steel yourselves for the battle yet to come. Support President Donald Trump, financially if you can, with messages to your elected representatives as in the one in the sidebar, get the message out to friends and family who you can influence or even just to lean on when you're getting down, and above all prayer. From where I sit now, this is far from over. Don't give in.

Tuesday, November 10, 2020

AG Billy the Bagpiper Barr[30] issued a memo stating that the DoJ will indeed be going forward with the investigation into the voter fraud of last Tuesday. That elicited the immediate resignation of an embedded blood-sucking tick by the name of Richard Pilger, a prosecutor who we find out was one of Lois Lerner's henchmen at the IRS who was persecuting conservative groups. And therein lies the problem; relying on institutions charged with upholding the law that are in and of themselves complicit in the criminality and corruption. While Barr himself elicits reactions from being incompetent all the way down to being in league with the coup plotters, I have very little faith that anyone at the DoJ will do their duty, and every reason to believe they will stonewall, slow-walk or sabotage this when time is of the essence. I'll take that stance and hope to be pleasantly surprised if they do indeed play against type.

On a hopeful note, and it's completely anecdotal, the more the media screams about Trump while making Biden's "win" a fait accompli, the more I get the sense that they know this might very well slip away from them. It's just a feeling, and I could be totally wrong. But as I have been saying since last week, my optimism is based on the things that are

---

30 AG William Barr

happening. And that includes multiple eyewitness accounts from postal workers and election workers in at least two states to massive fraud, as well as the forensic evidence that shows the 9:00PM switcheroo happening almost in real time, and most crucially – at least in Pennsylvania – the illegal actions that disempowered the state legislature from its authority to dictate election policy and rules in defiance now of at least one SCOTUS associate justice (Samuel Alito).

Elsewhere, the final batch of ballots I believe is still being counted in Arizona. Aside from the idiocy that election day was a week ago and that Florida, a state that has like twice the population of Arizona completed its count that night and certified the results, Trump might very well come close to Biden, and when the fraudulent ballots are chucked, overtake him and win the state. Then there's Georgia, where already the Democrats have gone from "not a smidgen of fraud!" to "well there might be some instances here and there but not enough to take the win away from Biden!" Again, that too was a state where Trump was well in the lead around 9:00PM and that's the time that the lights went out in Georgia. At least in Fulton County where like the other big blue shit-holes the count was stopped, the doors were sealed and the pallets o' ballots were trucked in.

And then there's the computer "glitches" in an election software that oddly enough was designed by a company connected to the Clinton Crime Family. A full manual recount – not a computer re-tabulation – should clearly expose the fraud. And considering these systems were in use in all the swing states, the vote count could very well swing back to where we saw it was going on Tuesday night: a decisive if not massive Trump victory.

Elsewhere, for those who need a little blood pressure spike this morning, Obama henchman Ben Rhodes and evidently Goofy Joey himself have been chatting away with foreign leaders and emissaries discussing all kinds of foreign policy goals and such. Aside from this being in clear violation of the Logan Act, it also is the same thing that the Deep Staters at the FBI and DoJ used as a pretext to set up and take down General Michael Flynn, a man whose used toilet paper these vermin are not even worthy to lick.

Anyway, we all know the score here. I will say that the almost hourly schizophrenia we're experiencing as we gasp at potentially horrendous news while then sighing with relief and joy when the tiniest bit of positive news comes our way is definitely taking a toll. But each day that passes where we don't lose any ground is good enough for me. I think yesterday was one of those days on multiple fronts. With any luck, today will be another one of those days, and so on and so on.

Aside from the court challenges, if/when Team Trump assembles and ultimately disseminates hard, cold evidence in all of its forms of the fraud in all of its forms, I hope that the state legislatures in the dirty half-dozen that are mostly if not all GOP-controlled, do their sworn Constitutional duty by recognizing that their elections were poisoned, and just go ahead and award President Trump its electors to the Electoral

College. Given the fact that the Democrat Party now has an armed militant wing in the form of Antifa/BLM, as well as other players such as would-be mass assassin James Hodgkinson who was and still is directly linked to Dick Durbin, the pressure on them to sit on their hands is understandably enourmous. There's also the message from the Democrat Party political and thought leadership (such as it is) that anyone who supported this president will face retribution. For these legislatures not to step up, even in the face of this, would be inexcusable given what's at stake; the fate of this republic here and now. It's a tall order to be sure but I believe the evidence is both massive and incontrovertible.

Wednesday, November 11, 2020

Well, the daily emotional rollercoaster ride of the 2020 election limbo continues. Yesterday started a bit down for me but it did end on a bit of an upswing thanks to several of the commenters who offered up insights and info, and not just empty (though always well-intentioned) cheerleading. The upswing continues this morning as, more and more, it looks like what happens in Pennsylvania is going to be the domino that will send the Democrat-Anti-Media Complex's plot to steal the election crashing down in ruins – – provided of course that those individuals who have the power and the duty to knock it down also have the moral fiber and the intestinal fortitude to do so.

As I said, the Keystone State is the key to this.[31]

"The Supreme Court ruled, sort of, in this case already. They said, with 4 Justices led by Justice Alito that ONLY the Pennsylvania legislature can make or modify voting rules. Read the opinions — this thing is NOT going to go to Biden.

It is black and white, in the United States Constitution, a dusty document tourists see in the National Archives in DC.

The Pennsylvania legislature did not allow such voting changes, the Pennsylvania Supreme Court, a quite partisan body, did. And the grown-ups at the U.S. Supreme Court said that was judicial overreach. That is not a good thing for Biden.

This week, Justice Alito again said all votes coming in after 8:00 PM on election night need to be segregated. That is what is called a Federal Court Order. That's no parking ticket.

The leftists will say this is a racist thing because of the word "segregated." Maybe separated would be more politically correct.

---

31 https://www.americanthinker.com/articles/2020/11/why_scott_adams_of_dilbert_fame_and_i_say_trump_wins_this_thing__bigly.html

Anyway, it is pretty clear with Justice Amy Barrett on the Supreme Court, those votes in Pennsylvania are getting backed out right after Rudy Giuliani makes his case. The mainstream media know that; thus, they are screwing with your heads and you are up all night eating popcorn looking for any shred of information. Go to sleep!"

The author goes on to assume that ultimately the Supreme Court will indeed rule to toss the Pennsylvania election on Constitutional grounds and then open the way for the state's legislature to award the 20 EVs to Trump, which then sets off a chain reaction in at least one or two other states and voila. While that is a possibility, and completely justified based on the evidence alone of the PA state court's usurpation of power, what is the probability of that happening? The Supreme Court of the United States disqualifying the results of state's votes in a national election – even one that on the evidence is open and shut – is to put it mildly a very tall order. Plus, given the extremely and openly partisan nature of the Chief Justice makes an already high hurdle become Everest on top of Olympus.

Meanwhile, a similar lawsuit concerning the unconstitutional disenfranchisement of an entire class of voters (meaning us) was filed in Michigan, along with the other lawsuits to halt the certification of the vote until the cases can be heard. Again, let me reiterate: on a purely legal and evidentiary basis, if President Trump for a moment thought that he was tilting at windmills, he would have conceded last week. I'm sure he fully understands the players involved here as well as the bar he has to pass, so to speak, in order to at a minimum make his case. Certainly, people such as Sidney Powell, Lin Wood and the others on his legal team are fully cognizant and have advised him as such. So at a minimum, you can be sure that they feel they have the goods and are preparing their case, knowing it has to be as solid and airtight as possible.

The other avenue of attack also involves the states' legislatures. As we all know, under Article II of the Constitution, they alone have the power to assign electors as they see fit. Given the fact that the Democrat Party now gives a nod and a wink if not open approval to acts of political terrorism to silence opposition, you have got to believe that the legislators in Pennsylvania and the other contested states do no relish the idea of a bullet in their eye or having to put out the flames on the backs of their kids. That is not hyperbole. See: James Hodgkinson.

Given that fact, the last thing I want to be right now is a Republican PA state legislator. But as someone who swore an oath to uphold the Constitution and the rights of the citizens of my state, there is no other option than to right the most egregious usurpation of power and crime in our history. To not do so is not just an abrogation of an oath, but it is to be complicit in the murder of our republic.

Thursday, November 12, 2020

Late yesterday, commenters had reported that the Enemy[32] in PA had destroyed the envelopes that allegedly contained questionable ballots, essentially making it impossible to distinguish between legitimate ones and fakes. Aside from spoliation of evidence, it amounts to the Enemy skywriting the words "Go Fuck Yourself!" in giant letters directly over the Supreme Court, after twice ignoring Justice Alito's order to segregate ballots that came in after 8:00PM on election night. The legalities of what it means, while not unimportant, are not relevant to this conversation. The message that it sends to the citizens of this country as well as the SCOTUS and the concept of the rule of law is quite clear. The question is, what are they and we going to do about it?

To be sure, I cannot imagine Justice Samuel Alito and at least three other Justices rolling over about this. That leaves John Roberts. Forgetting his hatred of this President, as well as his horrid track record in upholding the Constitution, what Roberts is constantly going on about is the preservation of the integrity of the Supreme Court (such as it is or was, if ever). These actions by the Enemy have got to be among the most egregious assaults on the Court, and the rule of law, in the nation's history, which if left unpunished will have come to an end as of November 3rd, 2020. If he or the others issue some sort of phony baloney wrist-slap while allowing the thievery to remain in place, then that will just confirm

---

32 My characterization of the Democrat-Media Complex

his spinelessness or phoniness, if not complicity. Trying to thread a needle as I imagine he may well be doing, while the Enemy is setting fire to your law library is beyond ridiculous at this point. I would hope the Chief Justice realizes what will happen to him and his precious Court if the nightmare scenario of losing the Presidency and the Senate comes to pass.

Then we have the GOP-controlled Pennsylvania legislature. What the Enemy has done to the court applies in equal terms to them. They are there to be a check on the power of the state's executive and judicial branches. Both have completely usurped their authority in illegally re-writing election laws and determining how elections are to be run. Forgetting the mountains of evidence proving the Enemy stole this election in Philadelphia and Pittsburgh, the usurpation of power to pull of that heist is, or at least should be, more than enough to stiffen the sinews and boil the blood of everyone in that legislature. Yes, I am very well aware of the physical danger each of them is in. But the only just recourse for them is to convene, declare the election intentionally sabotaged beyond repair by the Enemy and do their sworn duty to uphold the law by awarding the 20 electoral votes to President Trump. Considering that the race in the state was not exactly neck and neck – the President was ahead by over 600,000 votes with most of the precincts having reported in by 9:00PM on election night – should make this a no-brainer. Should.

That still leaves us with the other five stolen states. Georgia at least has authorized a full county-by-county audit and hand recount, even as the two Senate seats which were also stolen are now up for grabs in a runoff. Just as in PA, there are legal challenges coming in all of these places. But here again, all these states have GOP legislatures. While the cases are prepared and make their way inevitably to the courts, the aforementioned can put an end to this garbage here and now. Obviously, the political and societal consequences would be immediate and titanic.[33]

> *Screw the stats. Trump is the number-one communicator in this quadrant of the galaxy. Trump has scores of anecdotes like that loose string on the sock where, when you pull it a bit, the sock comes apart.*
>
> *The Trump rallies hit every swing state and educate their legislatures about the power of anecdotes. Anecdotes drive voters. Everyone remembers a story. Voters remember.*
>
> *This election must be certified by two chambers of every swing-state Legislature.*
>
> *The speaker in Pennsylvania just showed us the high ground. The Republican legislatures follow his lead and say no certification without the following:*
>
> *— a full audit, by hand of every vote*

33 https://www.americanthinker.com/articles/2020/11/the_real_election_trump_card_refuse_to_certify.html

— any court or election official mandate not approved by the Legislature does not count — take out those votes

— voting machines: cough up the source code, the audit logs for our forensic teams

You get the picture.

If the Democrats challenge this, the clock works against them. Thirty days. Tick, tick.

Trump plays the Trump card. Seventy-one million people demanding a recount — fair, honest, transparent.

No recount, no certification. No voting machine code review, no certification.

No certification, and the House of Representatives makes the call, and Trump gets off the golf course and back to work.

This is the high ground. The Democrats have given it to us; let us gather together and say "thanks."

Restoring this President for another term would invariably touch of a wave of violence and unrest not seen since the Civil War. Indeed, we are already in a state of civil war with the Enemy and have been to one degree or another for quite some time. The sad fact is, there is going to bloodshed in this country over who gets to decide its future; we who want to preserve it in its "as founded" state or the Enemy who seeks its dismantling and our subjugation or annihilation. If we lose this election the Enemy will no doubt remove more and more of our freedoms by shredding what's left of the Constitution, we lose more of the ability to resist.

It is far better now to endure the societal convulsions of restoring Trump to his rightful second term than the alternative. I pray to God in Heaven to give these flawed, justifiably terrified human beings on the bench and in the legislatures the courage to do what is right.

Monday, November 16, 2020

Saturday saw a massive pro-Trump "Million MAGA March" with tens of thousands of attendees flooding into DC, as well as smaller rallies elsewhere in the nation, including Milwaukee, one of the epicenters of the 6-state election theft. Naturally, the health department had to shut that one down because, virus! Back in DC, once again decent people got beaten up by the Enemy's Antifa/BLM goon squads while the police evidently let it happen, all because they had the gall to rise up in support of a president who represents them, literally and figuratively.

On the legal front, as Team Trump is doing whatever it can in the way of recounts and audits, the Enemy is now threatening those who would aid his cause. Evidently a second high-powered law firm has backed out of representing Trump's case in Pennsylvania. Over in Georgia, Brian Kemp and the GOP there are letting the Dems walk all over them in that state's recount, while the runoff election for the two Senate seats – no doubt in my mind stolen along with the President's electoral votes – ramps up. Fat fraud Tank Abrams is pimping mail-in ballots, and according to her about 600,000 have been sent out. To allow this insanity to happen yet again is just inexcusable. But I guess the Democrats run the show in that state so you're never going to beat the house. Feh. . .

. . . Honestly, I have no idea what the final outcome is going to be with this. My mood is swinging so wildly that I should look into getting a tank of lithium. If the nightmare scenario does come to pass, even with the incredible gains in the House or if the Enemy fail to rig and steal the two runoff Senate elections in Georgia, we face dictatorial decrees from whoever is controlling the Executive Branch and packed court or not, no one is going to stop them. Now we have these calls for unity, which is the moral equivalent of being forced to sing "Kumbaya" at gunpoint before we all get shot into a ditch.[34]

Political unity is an ugly, authoritarian idea. No free nation has domestic political unity, nor should it aspire to it.

---

34 https://nypost.com/2020/11/15/when-talk-of-unity-just-means-surrender/

What "unity" really means is capitulation. America is once again being subjected to the inane brand of pseudo-patriotic sloganeering we saw during President Barack Obama's tenure. Now, as then, the media will pretend that the moral fabric of the nation must be mended after GOP rule. It's pretty transparent.

When Dems win the presidency, we are treated to solemn calls for national restoration; the opposition must embrace decorum and pass legislation it opposes. When Republicans win elections, grown women put on knitted hats depicting their reproductive organs and stomp around DC protesting, all to media adulation...

...We do that sort of thing in Washington. The liberal pivot from #Resistance to "unity" is as swift as it is dishonest. After four years of treating every unexceptional conservative policy victory as one of the Seven Seals of the Apocalypse, Washington Post columnists are already dusting off their columns about "obstructionism" and "minority rule." After years of blanket opposition to Trump, we are being told that Joe Biden has a national "mandate."

He does not. G-d willing, Washington is headed for more "gridlock" — a completely healthy, organic reflection of the geographical, ideological and theo-

logical differences of real people in contemporary America. Congress makes laws, and right now, that institution is narrowly divided and unlikely to be able to come together on any of the big-ticket items Biden promised. This is why federalism exists.

Unity is found in comity with your neighbors, in your churches and schools, in your everyday interactions with your community. Politics is not a place for unity. It is a place for airing grievances. And we've got plenty.

Already, the knives are out for voices of dissent as we have seen with not only those protesting this "putsch" but on social(ist) media and the internet. The latest is WordPress has terminated its hosting agreement for Conservative Treehouse. With Rump Roast Clyburn[35] or something similar running the FCC, I don't even want to think about what will happen to the HQ. Or talk radio. A Biden flunky is already spouting garbage about the First Amendment being antiquated or some such rot...

...And while Wretched Whitmer[36] in Michigan has declared the state will once again be imprisoned on the pretext of the Chinese Lung AIDS[37], Dr. Scott Atlas had the 100% correct response:

---

[35] Former head of the FCC Mignon Clyburn, daughter of James Clyburn

[36] Michigan governor Gretchen Whitmer

[37] Chinese COVID-19

"The only way this stops is if people rise up.
You get what you accept. #FreedomMatters
#StepUp"

That has got to be the battle cry going forward. I hope and pray that Trump's victory is restored to him and we the people, whether via SCOTUS, the state legislatures or if it has to come down to it, the House. Obviously, the Enemy will not accept that. But if the reverse happens we cannot accept that. We have been forced by the Enemy down a dark path that started decades ago. I am not a deeply religious person but I am praying for some sort of Divine guidance as an individual but also as a nation. We sure could use a miracle right about now.

Wednesday, November 18, 2020

It serves me right going to bed last night thinking that maybe, just maybe, the good news out of Wayne County, MI was reason to keep hope alive. Instead, I wake up to my guts collapsing and my blood pressure rising.[38]

The Board of Canvassers had originally voted 2-2 along party lines. The tie meant the election results were not certified. But later into the night, the Republican canvassers flipped and voted with the Democrats, while the live video stream was down...

---

38 Chinese COVID-19

… With the certification by Wayne County, the results will now move to the State Board of Canvassers, which also has two Republicans and two Democrats as members.

Over 100 observers have filed affidavits related to the vote counting process in Detroit. Several individuals have alleged ballots being counted multiple times, ballots arriving in the dead of night, and observers being blocked from watching the tabulation process.

Of course Michigan's completely ethical, impartial, honest-as-the-day-is-long – and Nazi collaborator George Soros bought-and-paid-for – Secretary of State Jocelyn Benson has promised for a complete and fair audit of the results (puke). Look, we all know the score here; the race card aspect, as is always the case is total bullshit, especially in light of the fact that blacks and other minorities came out in record numbers all over the country to carry Trump on their shoulders to victory. It's those blacks who sure as hell are being disenfranchised with this garbage. In any case, being labeled with the race card I don't think necessarily entered into the calculus of the two GOP members of Wayne County's Board of Canvassers. More likely, Monica Palmer and William Hartmann were thinking about themselves and their families winding up in a morgue as victims of Chinese Lung AIDS or blunt force trauma, but mostly blunt force trauma.[39]

Of course as tantalizing as the original news was last night that to that point they were standing firm, at least the other Republican leaders in more solidly GOP counties in

---

39 https://amgreatness.com/2020/11/17/gop-board-of-canvassers-members-in-wayne-county-mi-cave-after-first-refusing-to-certify-2020-election-results/

the state will not be so easily swayed. Charlie Brown, Lucy, football...[40]

> *But that wasn't the end of the craziness coming out of Michigan. The State Senate Majority Leader, Mike Shrikey, a Republican, came down strongly on the side of... Joe Biden:*

> *Democrat Joe Biden is the president-elect, and while Michigan's Republican-led Legislature is investigating the election, it will not award the state's 16 electors to GOP President Donald Trump, Senate Majority Leader Mike Shirkey told Bridge on Tuesday.*

> *Hundreds of activists who protested at the Michigan Capitol on Saturday repeated the president's unproven claims of widespread voter fraud, urging lawmakers to "stop the steal" by choosing their own pro-Trump representatives to the Electoral College.*

> *Conservative groups have also started phone and letter-writing campaigns in an attempt to persuade legislative Republicans to decide the election for Trump.*

> *"That's not going to happen," Shirkey, R-Clarklake, said in a wide-ranging interview with Bridge Michigan. He noted state law awards electors to the winner of the state's popular vote. And Biden won*

40 https://www.americanthinker.com/blog/2020/11/the_michigan_gop_is_behaving_ strangely__and_very_badly.html

the state by more than 146,000 votes, according to unofficial results.

Well, what the actual fuck? For days now, a lot of people have been disparaging of Rudy Giuliani, Sidney Powell, Lin Wood and the rest of Team Trump. I am convinced more than ever that they have the evidence and most likely smoking gun evidence to prove that the results in all of the states in question were indeed tampered with, rigged and stolen via Dominion's election stealing software, thousands of phony mail-in ballots before November 3rd as well as the blatant ballot dumping and ejection of observers late that night. The problem was and remains very flawed individuals who either out of moral cowardice, duplicity with the Enemy, understandable fear for their and their families' personal safety or some combination of all of those, will not stand up and do their crystal clear duty and save the nation.

Thursday, November 19, 2020

I'm not going to get excited but it is nice to wake up to some good news in the morning and hopefully it won't be fleeting. The two Wayne County, Michigan GOP election canvassers who were subjected to naked terroristic threats and intimidation against them and their families are reportedly reversing their coerced votes to certify the county's election results. If this holds – IF – it is a very big deal. The report broke from Just The News:[41]

> *Their pronouncements come just 24 hours after a chaotic meeting in which the county's election board initially failed to certify the Nov. 3 election results during a 2-2 deadlocked vote when both Palmer and Hartmann voted against certification. But after hours of contentious public comment and criticism — including Democratic allegations of racism and threats against their safety — the two GOP members struck a deal to certify the elections in return for a promise of a thorough audit.*

> *Palmer and Hartmann said Wednesday they learned that state officials had reneged or would not honor the audit, leaving them no recourse but to oppose certification until more investigation could be performed.*

> *It was not immediately unclear[sic] whether the Tuesday night compromise was binding or could be changed, or whether the two members' decision to announce their rescinded votes would stop Michigan state officials from proceeding to name electors.*

41 https://justthenews.com/politics-policy/elections/wayne-county-election-board-republicans-say-they-were-bullied-rescind

*But both GOP board members said in the affidavits
they felt misled and unduly pressured to change their
positions the night earlier.*

One would think that a signature obtained under duress would be null and void, but given the state of our justice system, especially in jurisdictions controlled by the Enemy, I'm not so sanguine. But on the assumption that Palmer's and Hartmann's rescinding of their votes holds, the certification of the votes of Michigan's largest county cannot legally go forward. And as goes Wayne County, I assume so goes the rest of the state. Let's play this out a little further; if these individuals are acting just based on their own observations of Election Day, you have to wonder what their colleagues as well as the state legislators in Michigan will think when Team Trump officially presents its "kraken" of evidence to them and the courts. And then extrapolate that out to the other states in question.

But I think I am getting ahead of myself. The one very heartening thing that can't be taken away is the courage of Monica Palmer and Phillip Hartmann to do the right thing. The constant stream of incandescent vitriol being hurled at them about "racism" and "disenfranchising" blacks and minorities is a sick joke, considering Trump gained historic levels of black and minority votes all across the nation, and more than likely in Detroit, Atlanta, Philly, Pittsburgh and Milwaukee if we are ever able to toss the hundreds of thousands of fraudulent votes or ones switched via computer from Trump to Biden. As for this slug Abraham Aiyash who doxxed Monica Palmer's children, the book should thrown at him – or his house Rachel Corried – but that's not likely given the times we live in.[42]

In Georgia, unfortunately, the GOP there seems to be making a complete hash of the recount and audit. There is massive evidence of fraud, cheating and malfeasance yet the Secretary of State Brad Raffensperger goes on Fake Yapper's XiNN transmission to crow about his severe conservatism:[43]

> *"I've been a lifelong Republican," he said. "I'm a conservative Christian Republican. And you look at my voting record. I have been endorsed by pro-life business, pro-business groups, National Federation of Independent Businesses. I'm a business owner. And so, people say that I'm not Republican — it's crazy talk.*

That was after he proclaimed: ***"We have not seen any widespread voter fraud."***

You're a lifelong hack and jackass and Kelly Loefler is right; you should be shitcanned with extreme prejudice. Let's hope that we have more folks in the Georgia state legislature with the attitude of Palmer and Hartmann from Michigan than this fraud. If not, we got trouble in River City.

42 https://thefederalist.com/2020/11/18/michigan-democrat-doxxes-children-of-wayne-county-election-official/

43 https://www.breitbart.com/clips/2020/11/18/ga-secretary-of-state-raffensperger-biden-will-win-georgia-trump-hurt-chances-telling-people-not-to-vote-absentee/

Tuesday, November 24, 2020

The fallout if you will over Sidney Powell and both her non-official position on the Trump defense team and more crucially the veracity of her claims of election fraud is up front this morning. In the wake of Thursday's press conference that if nothing else was a giant morale booster for us, some on our side were less than impressed. Lots of smoke but no fire, so to speak. Most notably Tucker Carlson got into a heated exchange with Powell about her not revealing any of the evidence, which was bad enough. I know we all have our feelings about Carlson as well as the network he continues to get his paycheck from, and now providing the bulk of its revenue. But even Rush Limbaugh, while not necessarily telling her to shit or get off the pot, seemed to echo some frustration, insofar as you don't just have an hour long press event and not at least reveal at least something tangible. Yes, I realize that you don't show your hand to the Enemy before you make the actual case to whatever court or body that ultimately adjudicates this thing, legally and/or politically. Personally, I stand with Powell but just to play Devil's advocate, you don't strengthen your position by not giving us a reason to believe – aside from what we witnessed with our own eyes on election night and the following morning – as well as then being told that you are not working in any official capacity with the Trump Legal Team. Pedro Gonzalez at American Greatness:[44]

---

44 https://amgreatness.com/2020/11/23/truth-and-fraud-in-the-2020-election/

The issue with Powell was never that fraud didn't occur or that she was making it up out of whole cloth, but that her claims are so extraordinary that they would threaten to discredit the case for real fraud if they turned out to be exaggerated or in any way untrue. There are many compelling examples of irregularities involving mail-in ballots, ejected poll observers, and more that are worthy of serious investigating.

But Powell has set the bar so incredibly high above those things now. This is not to say that there is not or could not be some basic truth to some of her claims, but that it is dangerous to build the case for fraud entirely on one person's shoulders. As a result, "belief" in Powell has become a kind of purity test for some Trump supporters, creating internecine conflicts at the drop of a hat. It's also preventing the Trump movement from performing any kind of introspection on what might have been some of the campaign's mistakes.

If Powell's claims are all true, then there would be no need to consider that perhaps it was a mistake to court rather than tackle the corporate and tech forces now garroting Trump's last-ditch efforts. If Powell is right, there is no reason to criticize the Trump campaign's racial-spoils pandering, its failure to keep signature platform promises, or its critical personnel problems. Because the only problem will have been, according to her, that as many as 10 million fraudulent votes and up to 7 million votes were switched from Trump to Biden. The unexpected side effect of all this is an unremittingly uncritical movement that will circle the wagons to defend the most poisonous pills in the White House and viciously attack those who are otherwise allies. Powell's moment in the limelight is reminding us of the dangers of personality cults.

Aside from the idiotic line about "preventing the Trump movement from performing any kind of introspection on what might have been some of the campaign's mistakes" which when you strip away the fraud from the election, Trump ran a flawless campaign that would have won in as close to a landslide as we've had in decades, he does bring up valid points. It's not necessarily I think about Powell's integrity or the veracity of the charges, it's more about the degree of difficulty in proving them beyond any reasonable doubt in a court of law and most crucially, in the time remaining. That's some time between December 8th and 14th when the Electoral College convenes.

I have nothing but the greatest admiration for Sidney Powell. Her career, or to be more precise, the career with the globalists and corporatists that she rejected in favor of defending the principles of equal justice under a just and stable law from the depredations of the latter speaks volumes as to her character.[45]

If anyone doubts that there is not a Globalist plot to take America down, especially in light of what we and this President have experienced these past four to 20 years and really since the end of the Second World War, then please describe the bumps on your sigmoid as you have your head up your ass. If Sidney Powell is guilty of anything, it's perhaps fighting the right battle but at the wrong time. That is unless she really does have the Kraken of all evidence ready to be released. I hope she does. In any case, my anger is not at her, nor at Rudy Giuliani, Jenna Ellis or anyone else on the Trump Team. My incandescent rage that can never be slaked is at the traitors and the Enemy for snuffing out the last vestige of this republic and for those allegedly on our side who are their willing accomplices. Worst of the bunch are the state legislators and other GOP politicians in the six states that know firsthand that the Enemy stole their elections and should be convening right now to assign their electors to Trump. There is no excuse for that, threats of violence or not. This is a war now, and we are this close to an open shooting war, and considering the firebombing of several dozen cities over the past six months, arguably we're at that stage already.

Whatever happens with Sidney Powell's case, she is the very last person I am ever going to attack. For me, her motivations, if not perhaps (as remains to be seen) her strategy, are beyond reproach. Until you (the royal you) show me the

45 https://stream.org/i-know-sidney-powell-she-is-telling-the-truth/

proof – as you have demanded of her – that she is anything but a great patriot, I'm with her all the way. Because we are going to need an army of Sidney Powell's should worse come to worse.

Wednesday, November 25, 2020

With the day before Thanksgiving upon us, the news seems to be getting more dispiriting and disheartening as time goes on. No, I'm not giving up hope that somehow Trump will prevail, but the direct political descendants of those who unleashed Kolyma, Birkenau and the Killing Fields are in the ascendancy right here regardless of who is sworn in this coming January 20th. We dodged a bullet to the neck and a tumble into the figurative (and perhaps literal) mass grave four years ago, and had history repeated itself, as it most certainly was going to until a water main break in an Atlanta basement somehow caused six states to vault Polident-Elect Biden into the lead, it only would have bought us maybe four more years of a reprieve. No doubt with double the impeachment hearings, double the foney-Phlu[46] lockdowns and worst of all, double the duplicitousness of an alleged opposition party that is completely dead to me, but a reprieve nonetheless.

Let's face reality; Sinclair Lewis' It Can't Happen Here has happened here.[47] America as founded, as we had imagined or

---

46 Chinese COVID-19

47 https://www.amazon.com/Cant-Happen-Here-Signet-Classics/
dp/0451465644

perhaps deluded ourselves into thinking it was, was snuffed out on November 3rd. We can thank President Trump for that, and I'm not at all being sarcastic. In fact, it's probably the greatest achievement of his presidency. By being an outsider and refusing to be subsumed by a sea of corruption and criminality whose purpose was – is – the generational enterprise of dismantling this country and our society and delivering its corpse to a Globalist cabal with Communist China on top, he forced its agents to reveal themselves for who and what they are to a heretofore mostly unaware citizenry. The domestic and foreign policies that he was able to enact, with virtually zero help if not resistance from the late GOP, not only were triumphs but served to underscore what complete and disastrous failures the self-proclaimed Ivy League, Skull and Bones, internationalist "elites" had been strangling us with since the end of the Second World War. And he rubbed their faces in it on Twitter with exclamation points.

Yes, we are not just in a post-Constitutional America but we are on the verge of being in a post-America America. The question therefore is, Trump or no Trump, what are we going to do about it? With virtually every political, legal, academic and cultural institution now thoroughly corrupted, there's nowhere to turn. And as was made abundantly clear three weeks ago, we're not voting our way out of this. I'm sorry if I'm being depressive, especially on the eve of a day when we traditionally give thanks to G-d for both the blessings of our table and for the ability to live in freedom. Well, now that's all shot to hell, isn't it?

As Thomas Paine wrote, *"THESE are the times that try men's souls. The summer soldier and the sunshine patriot will, in this crisis, shrink from the service of their country; but he that stands it now, deserves the love and thanks of man and woman.*

Tyranny, like hell, is not easily conquered; yet we have this consolation with us, that the harder the conflict, the more glorious the triumph.

What we obtain too cheap, we esteem too lightly: it is dearness only that gives every thing its value. Heaven knows how to put a proper price upon its goods; and it would be strange indeed if so celestial an article as FREEDOM should not be highly rated."

And finally, I'll leave you with Psalm 121: *"I will lift up mine eyes unto the hills, from whence cometh my help. My help cometh from the LORD, which made heaven and earth."*

Stay strong, have faith and never give up hope. We're still here.

Tuesday, December 1, 2020

On a positive note, it looks as if three more House seats will go our way with incumbents Lee Zeldin in NY and Mike Garcia in CA officially winning re-election and Claudia Tenney, also in NY, holding on by just 13 votes in what I believe is the final recount. Funny how Republicans were supposed to have been wiped out in a so-called Blue Wave while up and down the ticket it's the Democrats that got crushed. At least everywhere where they couldn't steal the election.

That of course segues into the presidential election where even as more evidence of the initial plot as well as the last minute, six-state smash and grab massive ballot dumping is exposed, the rush to cover it all up and just declare Polident-Elect Joey Shin-Splint[48] the winner is in full force. Sadly, tragically, the GOP is aiding and abetting this farce when every last Congressman, Senator, all the way on down to local Dog Catcher should be screaming bloody murder in unison. Moreover, it's the state legislators who can remedy this situation immediately by assigning their electors to Donald Trump. It never ceases to amaze me that no matter how obvious, open and outrageous the infamy perpetrated on the American people, the more blind to it that those on our side become, as well as indignant at us for pointing it out to them. The myth that the Democrat Party and its Greek chorus media propaganda wing – The Enemy – are the "loyal opposition" was exploded long ago, along with the illusion that our political system is operating under anything even remotely resembling regular order. That should've been obvious after Dick Durbin's friend James Hodgkinson shot up Steve Scalise and several others, or when Rand Paul's neighbor speared him in the back and on and on and on. But still they persisted… in saying and doing nothing.

---

48 President-elect Joe Biden

That brings us to the courts, and ultimately the Supreme Court. That is if time doesn't run out.[49]

We now have strong evidence of massive electoral fraud. Crimes were committed. There is a limited amount of time to correct the matter. State legislatures are holding hearings and might save the republic by awarding electors to the candidate who in fact did get the most votes in their respective states.

Whether they do or not, the question remains: can the courts restrict themselves to the narrowest interpretation of the law, without regard for the consequences — the consequences of permitting the presidency to be occupied by the favored candidate of a massive criminal enterprise? Can they ignore the strong likelihood that a Biden presidency (followed within days or weeks by a Harris presidency) will open the floodgates of illegal immigration? Can they ignore the evidence that the Democrats will award citizenship to millions of them? Can they avert their gaze from a future in which the levers of power will be controlled by a party that can illegally ensure never losing another election? Can the Supreme Court, indeed, disregard that it will soon be swamped by additional justices who will impose socialism on the nation?

---

49 https://www.americanthinker.com/blog/2020/11/will_the_courts_help_america_on_the_road_to_suicide.html

In other words, will the criminals be set free to perpetuate their crimes? Will the Republic itself be murdered?

It can be argued that none of this is any business of the Supreme Court, and in ordinary times, that would be correct — but these are not ordinary times. It has been said that "the Constitution is not a suicide pact."

We may be about to find out.

And therein lies the rub, regardless of the outcome, or actually if indeed Trump does prevail and the nation holds on for four more years. When one side not only no longer plays by the rules but is supported by a large percentage of people that views the nation itself as illegitimate and those who support it as an evil to be eradicated, then there is no nation, regardless of who is president. How are President Trump, if he is vindicated, please G-d, and the rest of us supposed to live under these conditions when a third or more of the populace want us dead? Any move to eradicate the cancer that is the left – be it in politics, the bureaucracy, academia or wherever – will instantly be met by those who seek to destroy the Constitution hiding behind it while trying to burn its last remaining shred.

In more ways than one, we are definitely not voting our way out of this. I am scared shitless for the future, but at the same time I am angry beyond my capacity to describe it. All

I can say is G-d help these bastards. One day, there will be a comeuppance. His will be done.

Thursday, December 3, 2020

Yesterday, the President gave "the most important speech" of his life, in describing what he and we believe to be the greatest crime in American history; the theft of a national presidential election.[50]

The president explained that our once-sacred "election day" has turned into an election season, with opportunities for "lots of bad things." While he was warned away from declaring a "premature victory," Biden was treated as the victor before the election happened. "In fact, they were acting like they already knew what the outcome was going to be. They had it covered and perhaps they did, very sadly for our country."

Trump assured his supporters, though, that he will keep fighting, using the "constitutional process." He explained that the fight was necessary because the election was corrupt.

Democrats engaged in a "relentless push to print and mail out tens of millions of ballots sent to unknown

---

50 https://www.americanthinker.com/blog/2020/12/trump_gave_the_most_important_speech_of_his_life.html

*recipients with virtually no safeguards of any kind,"
which was a petri dish for fraud...*

*... Given the overwhelming direct evidence and
indicia of fraud, the only way to save the system is
to overturn the election, "because our country cannot
live with this kind of an election." A revolt is unlikely
because Trump's votes are real, so his huge pool of supporters will be happy. Biden had many fewer votes
than he now claims, lowing the risk of unrest.*

*The "entrenched interests" behind this fraud, whom
(significantly) he does not name, "oppose our
movement because we put America first. They don't
put America first, and we're returning power to you
the American people. They don't want America first,
they only want power for themselves."*

*Trump wrapped up by urging the necessity of reviewing
the evidence of fraud, not just for his benefit, but for
America's good. Without election integrity, we don't
have a viable country. Biden, therefore, should also
want an investigation. "Ultimately, I am prepared
to accept any accurate election result, and I hope that
Joe Biden is as well."*

The evidence from the circumstantial to the physical to
eyewitness testimony to open and shut matters of unconstitutional actions by state politicians and courts is IMHO

overwhelming. At the very least, taken in toto, it calls into serious doubt the outcome in at least the 6 contested swing states and perhaps a number of others that went to the Enemy camp. The only question is the nature of the spine and moral character of the individuals who will make the final call. Sadly, if past performance is any predictor of future action, I am not filled with strength and confidence that said individuals will do what is not only justified but required.

Meanwhile, as we writhe in metaphorical agony on the ground waiting for death, two more shining examples of character, virtue and integrity have stepped up to defecate in our mouths.[51]

> *Sen. Mike Lee (R-UT) is expected to seek Senate passage of his S.386 job-outsourcing bill Wednesday evening.*
>
> *If no Republican or Democrat objects to Lee's actions, his bill will pass the Senate by so-called "Unanimous Consent," (UC), setting the stage for a joint House-Senate conference to draft a final bill.*
>
> *Lee's aggressive effort to pass the bill by UC is a threat to the GOP Senators and their slim majority, an immigration activist told Breitbart News. "They have to give Georgia Republicans a reason to vote*

---

51 https://www.breitbart.com/immigration/2020/12/02/mike-lee-to-seek-senate-approval-of-his-s-386-outsourcing-bill/

[in January] — and UC for this bill ain't that," the activist said.

Lee is trying to pass the bill after Sen. Rick Scott (R-FL) dropped his opposition to the legislation.

. . . I am sick to death of these people. Time and time again, they have proven themselves worse than useless; they have proven themselves to be frauds that are in league with the destruction of this nation and republic. What the actual hell are we fighting for? Our government is corrupt, our courts are corrupt, our media is corrupt, our schools are corrupt, our religious institutions are corrupt and our culture is corrupt. To coin a favorite slogan of The Enemy which is nevertheless appropriate, we're alone in this together.

Maybe that is the key here insofar as a movement of true national resistance and rebirth because this cannot go on. Whatever happens come January 20th, 2021, we are all Donald Trump now.

Friday, December 4, 2020

The most dispiriting news has been the infighting on our side centered around the two Georgia Senate seats that are up for grabs vis a vis backing two candidates whose conservative bona fides are perhaps dubious at best. Maybe if every GOP Senator and Congressman walked out en masse from both chambers, gathered at the White House lawn with the President, joined by the GOP state legislators in the six "contested" states and announced on camera that the 2020 election was stolen by the Democrats and that it was their intention to award their electors to Donald Trump, it might make me a tad more enthusiastic about keeping the Senate in Republican control.

But instead of doing what I mentioned above, what did the GOP-controlled Senate do? They stabbed the American people in the face by voting against a central pillar of President Trump's agenda, border and immigration control. I get it, we all get it; Democrats controlling the Senate, House and White House means lights out America forever. But when Mike Lee and the other traitors do this to us, it's kind of difficult for me to get it up for Loeffler and Perdue. And this is not just one issue. This has been the track record of the GOP going back into the Obama years if not further. "We're only three-fifths of two-thirds of on-half of government! Just give us the majority!" How'd that work out for us, specifically the first two years of President Trump's first term?

Yes, we need to control the Senate for all the obvious reasons. But choosing between tyrannical Communist, anti-Semitic, anti-Christian America-hating thugs and criminals or the grifters with the GOP label who make their money playing the fool for the latter whilst aiding and abetting in the dismantling of the nation is Hobsonian at best. Whatever Lin Wood and Sidney Powell are thinking in attacking Perdue and Loeffler, I really do not want to hear Newt Gingrich lecturing us on how that is unhelpful, especially after the precious GOP Senate majority moved ahead at warp speed to open the borders and fuck over the American worker – yet again. And then there's Pee-Air Defecto:[52]

"Well, the attorney general has said there's no there, there. The courts have all looked at the evidence and said there's no evidence there. Now, of course, there will be circumstances where one or two, or a handful, maybe even 100 ballots were incorrectly sent in or counted, and those things get adjusted and get fixed, but the idea of widespread fraud is simply not been shown to us. And if that evidence does exist, please show it to us."[53]

Mitt Romney: you, sir, are scum. The sight of you, the sound of your voice and the mere mentioning of your accursed name induce a gag reflex and violent retching. Oh to hear the children laugh and sing when one day, hopefully soon, the announcement of your death makes the headlines.

Now that I have vented my spleen, it's funny that the previously named rat in question talks about showing the evidence. It's there, evidently caught on tape along with eyewitness testimony from people that are being threatened with and have had actual physical violence visited upon them for coming forward. And just like the first failed coup attempt with the Russia Collusion Hoax/Impeachment Pretext, the more evidence that piled up proving it to be a hoax and that Obama, Clinton et al abused our law enforcement and national security apparatus (with their willing help) to

---

52 Pierre Delecto, AKA Sen Mitt Romney

53 https://www.breitbart.com/clips/2020/12/03/romney-trumps-election-fraud-claims-damaging-america-biden-will-be-president-january-20/

engineer it, the more that comes to light, the more strident is its dismissal and sweeping under the rug.

I'm not going to speculate now on what may or may not happen in the Supreme Court, the state legislatures or perhaps ultimately in the House of Representatives. Well over 74 million Americans have had one of their most precious rights, one central to the very existence of this republic itself – the right to have an honest vote – taken away from them. This on top of the right to worship as, when and how they choose, the right to voice an opinion freely without fear of retribution and the right to earn a living taken from them all on the pretext of a phony health crisis, combined with the mere fact that tech moguls and others control the means of discourse.

This cannot go on. This must not go on. Either there will be justice or there will be retribution. Right now, I'm in the mood for the latter.

Tuesday, December 8, 2020

While Sidney Powell's lawsuits in both Georgia and Michigan have been out of hand by those states' corrupt federal courts, Texas has slammed those two states plus Pennsylvania and Wisconsin with a suit at the Supreme Court.[54]

Texas is asking the Supreme Court to order the states to allow their legislatures to appoint their electors. The lawsuit says:

54 https://www.breitbart.com/politics/2020/12/07/texas-sues-georgia-michigan-pennsylvania-and-wisconsin-at-supreme-court-election-rules/

Certain officials in the Defendant States presented the pandemic as the justification for ignoring state laws regarding absentee and mail-in voting. The Defendant States flooded their citizenry with tens of millions of ballot applications and ballots in derogation of statutory controls as to how they are lawfully received, evaluated, and counted. Whether well intentioned or not, these unconstitutional acts had the same uniform effect — they made the 2020 election less secure in the Defendant States. Those changes are inconsistent with relevant state laws and were made by non-legislative entities, without any consent by the state legislatures. The acts of these officials thus directly violated the Constitution.

Texas approached the Supreme Court directly because Article III provides that it is the court of first impression on subjects where it has original jurisdiction, such as disputes between two or more states.

Along with the angles being pursued by Sidney Powell and Lin Wood, the official Trump legal team is making hay while it can in a parallel full-court press on the state legislatures themselves to recognize the massive and coordinated fraud pre-Election Day and the night of, when the counting stopped and the ballots were dumped, along with all the other evidence both solid and circumstantial as reason to invoke their Article II authority in awarding the electors.[55]

---

55 https://pjmedia.com/election/tyler-o-neil/2020/12/07/jenna-ellis-swing-state-legisla-tures-will-reject-false-corrupt-results-switch-electors-to-trump-n1196516

This legislative approach represents another facet of the Trump team's push to reverse the allegedly tainted results. "We do have the parallel paths. We are continuing on in the judiciary and I do anticipate that we will get to the Supreme Court," Ellis told Fox Business's Charles Payne. The legislative approach represents an alternate path to the same result.

Ellis said she and former New York Mayor Rudy Giuliani have been "going to the state legislators and telling them that they actually have the constitutionally-delegated authority to make sure that they select their delegates in the manner that does not allow for corruption."

"When all of these rules and laws in these states have been ignored, it's actually their constitutional obligation, responsibility, and exclusive power to make sure that they take back their delegates and they don't allow these false certifications to move forward," the Trump lawyer argued.

Ellis predicted that the legislatures of Arizona, Georgia, Pennsylvania, and Michigan would use their authority over determining Electoral College electors in order to reverse the fraud which Ellis argued was responsible for Biden's margin in those states.

I am heartened by her confidence, and the evidence is both massive and solid, but it's arguably an extremely tough row to hoe. And with a nation that is on the verge of an actual shooting civil war, the consequences to those charged with doing their Constitutional duty are obvious. That said, there are some legislators in a few of the states that are now openly questioning the validity of the elections in their states as well as the rush to certify them, choose the electors and legitimize the steal. No doubt this ultimately is going to go to the Supreme Court but it's extremely long odds that that body is going to actually decide the case, much preferring to send it back down to the States to adjudicate the matter. Not that I'm making a prediction but if – and it's a very big if – the Court were to rule, I think the pivotal player may turn out to be Samuel Alito. It was Alito who was told go fuck yourself, twice, by Pennsylvania's Democrat machine when they were ordered to segregate the ballots that came in after election day, and then spoliated the evidence by destroying the accompanying envelopes to prevent any sort of accurate accounting. I do not think that has gone done well with the esteemed associate justice, who heads up that state's area in cases that come before the court (he's also bumped up the deadline from Wednesday to today for that state's crooks to respond to the case). While John Roberts hates Trump's guts, he's such a raving egomaniac that he might actually join the majority just so that he could write what would be one of, if not the most important opinion in US history. But this is getting WAY ahead of things.

Wednesday, December 9, 2020

Yet again, our guts are being taken for a ride as we go from promising news to disappointing and/or bad news about the ultimate outcome of the theft of the election. . . Whatever the legal as well as the political aspects of attempting to secure redress via regular order there are, the situation we find ourselves in has gone way beyond anything in our history.

It's particularly infuriating to me that the easiest, or at least the clearest most obvious recourse in all of this is the GOP-controlled state legislatures doing their duty by invoking Article II and awarding their electors to President Trump. Failing that, they can or at least should refuse to certify their elections and throw it to the House of Representatives. But with a combination of fear of physical violence against them and their families or worse, collusion with the Chinese-controlled Democrat-Enemy, they are trying to fob off their duty on someone else. They swore the same oath to the Constitution that anyone in uniform does, and it carries with it every bit of the same weight. I don't give a flying fig about what BLM and Antifa might do to them or the Democrat shit-holes that caused this situation. Your duty is clear. Your moral failing and cowardice even clearer. I cannot describe for you how hateful that is.

Circling back to the initial gut punch, yesterday evening the news broke that SCOTUS has refused to hear the lawsuit challenging the election results in Pennsylvania. Particularly disturbing was that the decision was unanimous. Hello? Justice Alito? Ted Cruz reacted:[56]

"I'm disappointed that the Court decided not to hear the case challenging the election results in Penn-

sylvania. The anger and division we see across the Nation needs resolution. Late last year, the Pennsylvania Legislature passed a law that purported to allow universal mail-in voting, notwithstanding the Pennsylvania Constitution's express prohibition. This appeal filed raised important and serious legal issues, and I believe the Court had a responsibility to ensure our elections follow the law and the Constitution."

My rebuke for the state legislators above is directed in equal measure for the Supreme Court. Some have suggested that perhaps this is maneuvering on Alito's part to clear the way for the suit brought by the state of Texas, and now with a number of other states joining in as co-plaintiffs, which encompasses not only Pennsylvania but seeks to overturn the theft in Michigan, Georgia and Wisconsin as well. Forgetting Roberts or even Gorsuch, it is unfathomable to me that individuals like Clarence Thomas, Samuel Alito and Amy Coney Barrett would refuse to hear a case like this that is clear, unambiguous and historic in its magnitude and implication. The fact that there has been radio silence from the bench about why they refused to hear it makes it that much more frustrating.

Yet on the positive side, there is the lawsuit from Texas et al against PA, GA, MI and WI (Pagamiwi?) that the court must hear. And it's a doozy.[57]

---

57 https://www.americanthinker.com/blog/2020/12/the_texas_lawsuit_in_the_supreme_court_is_huge.html

The Texas lawsuit argues that the four defendant states changed their mail-in voting rules without going through the constitutional, legislative process. By doing so, they assured illegal mail-in votes, meaning all votes under the new "rules" were illegal from the get-go. These invalid votes override the will of those who legitimately cast votes, tainting the national election.

After all, we are a federation of states. While the individual states control their own election rules, each state is affected by the election outcomes in the other states. Texas Attorney General Ken Paxton's statement about the lawsuit perfectly sums up the correct legal standard:

> "Trust in the integrity of our election processes is sacrosanct and binds our citizenry and the States in this Union together. Georgia, Michigan, Pennsylvania and Wisconsin destroyed that trust and compromised the security and integrity of the 2020 election. The states violated statutes enacted by their duly elected legislatures, thereby violating the Constitution. By ignoring both state and federal law, these states have not only tainted the integrity of their own citizens' vote, but

of Texas and every other state that held lawful elections," said Attorney General Paxton.

"Their failure to abide by the rule of law casts a dark shadow of doubt over the outcome of the entire election. We now ask that the Supreme Court step in to correct this egregious error."

Because this is a suit between two states, the Supreme Court has original jurisdiction. It's also a factually pure case, that does not require looking at the reams of evidence demonstrating fraud…

No wonder it appears that eight other states have joined the case (Arkansas, Florida, Louisiana, Mississippi, Alabama, Kentucky, North Carolina, and South Carolina). The only thing that remains to be seen is whether the Supreme Court justices are willing to show the necessary courage to ensure that the will of the people, and not the will of the corruptocrats, prevail in this election.

Bingo. Again, the physical evidence, the eyewitness testimony, the digital forensic evidence, the circumstantial evidence and all the rest of it – when given a thorough review with an open mind – is incontestable. But as I have postulated about similar situations in the past, it seems as if the more clear and solid the case the more apt those who must make the right decision do the exact opposite. I hope to G-d

I'm wrong here. John Roberts supposedly considers it his mission to preserve the integrity and alleged impartiality of the Supreme Court. If he fails and then we lose the two seats in Georgia (also no doubt stolen five weeks ago), then he can kiss the integrity of the Court goodbye along with any power or influence he wields on it. Kind of ironic that in order to keep himself relevant, he has to save the presidency of a man he personally hates.

I stated above, whatever is happening here is far outside the scope of anything even approaching the ordinary. Yet the legislators, the justices and as a last resort Congressmen still have the power and authority to do their duty and restore justice. If they are collectively or individually trying to perform some sort of Solomonic miracle with a scalpel, they're wasting their time. What is needed here is an Excalibur-sized terrible swift sword of Justice. I pray to G-d that He opens these people's minds and stiffens their backbones.

Otherwise, it's going to be a very long and dark night.

Thursday, December 10, 2020

The big story is the Texas lawsuit against the four states where the Democrats stole the election. There are now 18 states that have joined Texas in the suit, which due to the nature of it being one or more states suing others means it goes straight to the Supreme Court for some sort of adjudication.[58]

58 https://www.americanthinker.com/articles/2020/12/a_summary_of_texas_election_lawsuit_.html

Significant violations of election law that were put into place to protect against election fraud is suffi-cient to invalidate the results of the elections, apart from whatever evidence is able to be gathered in a short time to show actual numbers of fraudulent ballots. Reason would indicate that there is a high number of fraudulent ballots that are impossible to identify, which is why the election laws pertaining to mail-in ballots were established to begin with.

There is no remedy to correct the Nov 3rd election because ballots that did not adhere to election law cannot be identified as separate from those that did. An accurate count of legal ballots that were cast cannot be made. Therefore, as directed in the Consti-tution, it falls to the legislature of each state to choose electors as has been done in the past. Failing that, each state may determine not to submit any presi-dential electors.

The Texas lawsuit claims the odds of Biden overcom-ing Trump's lead and winning any of the states after the point indicated was one in a quadrillion. And therefore, the odds of winning all four was one in a quadrillion to the fourth power. The lawsuit did not provide information on how that number was determined. This may seem an exaggerated to some. It is enough to state that the odds of winning any one of the states was highly unlikely and the odds of winning all four were extremely unlikely...

... But even if the odds were orders of magnitude better than that, they were still astronomically small. At any rate, the merits of the lawsuit do not depend on any certain level of odds of Biden overcoming a lead that had been established by 3:00 A.M. the day after election.

The other salient point not quoted above is the fact that election laws were changed by the judicial and/or executive branches in each of the states in direct contravention of the Constitution and violation of state laws; only the states' legislative branches have the authority to do so. It was an incontestable, flagrant violation that at a minimum should disqualify the results and if not lead to SCOTUS deciding in favor of Trump by awarding him the electors (highly unlikely), then revoking any certification of the elections and instructing the states' legislatures to award their electors as they see fit.

And this, as we all are well aware by now, leads to the very big question marks of how will SCOTUS rule in this, perhaps the most significant case in US history since Dred Scot if not ever, and if they do in fact throw it back to the legislatures their rulings. It is highly unlikely that SCOTUS itself will directly rule to award the electors to Trump, but that they will in fact recognize that the elections were indeed compromised as well as unconstitutional insofar as the flagrant usurpation of the state legislatures' supremacy in making election law and then throw it back to them. Their options are to assign electors in a manner of their choosing or refuse to assign any. By doing that, if the final tally leaves neither Trump nor the Polident-elect with 270 electoral votes, it goes to the House of Representatives who then get to decide who will be the next President. And that vote is by number of states, not representatives. I believe the split is 26-24 in favor of the GOP...

...The nation is literally on the brink of extinction. Then again, even if Trump had emerged or please G-d winds up emerging victorious, the same rot that has corrupted our government, society and culture will still exist and pose an existential threat well beyond 2024. On a positive note, I think Trump has caused a great awakening that is not going to go away whatever the outcome of this election is. If nothing else, he has exposed the menace of the globalist anti-American project that has been eating away at us since the end of the Second World War, if not since Wilson. Even the least informed person who is not a brain-dead Marxist understands something is terribly wrong, and it's neither Trump nor his policies. I could care fuck all about the GOP and all this talk about what it needs to do and all that other rot presupposing that party's relevancy, when it is in fact dead or worse, an undead zombie co-conspirator with The Enemy.

We are in a civil war for this nation. It either gets somewhat easier with Trump still at the helm or exponentially more difficult with him out of office, and perhaps nothing to stop The Enemy from having its way with us. Except mass and sustained civil disobedience or worse, armed insurrection. I am praying it never comes to that, but given everything we have seen so far, to dismiss out of hand that that is a distinct possibility is to be living in denial. Between China and Iran abroad and our own homegrown rabid Maoists and their Big Tech, Wall Street, CoC[59] enablers at home, I'm scared shitless. If worse comes to worse, I'll figure it out.

Monday, December 14, 2020

Today is the day that the Electoral College is supposed to convene and elect the next president. While what SCOTUS did on Friday in refusing to even hear the case (as the two justices who voted in favor of hearing the case, Alito and Thomas, have so far remained silent as to why) there is still a tiny flicker from a candle in a drafty room, but with an open jerry can full of 100 octane only a few tantalizing inches away.[60]

The Texas suit, later joined by other states, against Wisconsin, Pennsylvania, Michigan, and Georgia, was a nice try, but it was always a long shot. Of course SCOTUS would be reluctant to grab so much power by ordering state legislatures to seat the right

---

59 US Chamber of Commerce

60 https://www.americanthinker.com/articles/2020/12/we_dont_need_scotus_to_win.html

electors. Why? Because the power is already in the hands of the legislatures to do this...

...The undisputed states vote electorally on Dec. 14, and neither Biden nor Trump reaches 270, so neither one is the winner. The five GOP state legislatures (Arizona, Michigan, Georgia, Wisconsin, and Pennsylvania) of the six disputed states (minus Nevada) say they need to postpone their electoral votes because they are investigating fraud and illegalities. The legislatures perform due diligence (they have been holding hearings to collect the evidence) and conclude that fraud and illegalities unilaterally hurt Trump and helped only Biden. Assuming that the Democrat Legislature in Nevada says everything was legitimate, each disputed GOP state may reach this conclusion on any day after Dec. 14 -- say, on Dec. 27 or even Jan. 15. Then they appoint electors who vote for the rightful winner: Trump (provided the GOP-selected electors do not suffer from TDS). These votes are added in to the votes cast on Dec. 14. Trump goes past 270 electoral votes. He wins!

However, what happens if the disputed states cannot select the electors, and neither Trump [nor] Biden reaches 270? Then it goes to the House of Representatives, and each state has one vote, and this one vote is determined by the political makeup of the state legislatures. The GOP controls 29 state legislatures, and the Democrats have 19 (two are split). Trump wins again.

Therefore, we don't need SCOTUS to win, and we never needed it.

While this rationale is nothing new, it does bear repeating. Unfortunately, the rubber meets the road when even the most clear cut and justified procedures come up against the reality of human weakness. Threats of violence and other depredations and persecution don't exactly help matters either. Aside from the BLM-tifa black-clad brown-shirts, we have low scum in high places like this Cynthia Johnson from Michigan and now Congressthug Bill Pascrell (D)-Simone, calling for actual purges.[61]

Following the Supreme Court's denial of the Texas lawsuit -- later joined by 17 states, New Jersey Democrat Rep. Bill Pascrell is demanding that House Speaker Nancy Pelosi refuse to seat the 126 House Republicans who supported the Texas suit.

[Legal Insurrection] readers may recall Pascrell filing complaints against and trying to get lawyers representing President Trump disbarred.

---

61 https://legalinsurrection.com/2020/12/democrat-nj-rep-demands-pelosi-not-seat-126-gop-reps-who-backed-texas-suit/

Invoking the 14th Amendment regarding the disqualification from public office of anyone "engaged in insurrection or rebellion," Pascrell asserts that these Republicans committed "unbecoming acts that reflect poorly on our chamber" and as such should not be seated.

To no one's surprise, Pascrell's equally TDS-deranged fellow traveler and socialist "Squad" member Minnesota Rep. Ilhan Omar backs this ludicrous (and not a little ironic) demand that Representatives be barred from taking the office to which they were duly elected by voters in their districts.

It never ceases to amaze - and infuriate - me that the Enemy always accuses and blood libels us with the very things that they are guilty of. What Pascrell says is akin to the victim of a violent gang rape being told it was her fault for dressing provocatively while walking in a neighborhood she was warned to avoid. These people are playing with fire. Whatever happens comes January 20th, 2021, there are 80 million of us who voted for President Trump, and probably upwards of at least double that who support him and/or do not want whatever is left of this republic to be wiped out. We are not going anywhere. And we are enraged. When people like Allen West are now openly talking about secession, it would behoove Pascrell et al to shut their cake holes long enough to contemplate their words and deeds. Considering who and what they are, I think that that is a non-starter.

Wednesday, December 16, 2020

I don't have the energy to be either hopeful or depressed by whatever the latest news may be in terms of Trump and all of us overcoming the overthrow of the legitimate government of the United States by a treasonous domestic enemy, no doubt aided and abetted by one or more foreign ones. I only know that no matter what transpires on January 20th, 2021, this nation has been changed forever. That is inarguable, irrespective of whatever tripe the professional propagandists or the average brain dead lefty might spout.

G-d bless Rush Limbaugh, last week he broached the rather controversial subject of national divorce on his show, and the vermin with press credentials went ape. Let me backtrack and state that were this any other time, even perhaps during the Obama reign of error, it would be controversial. Today, all things considered, it's not only not controversial, but given the words, deeds, history and promises/threats of the American Left, I'd go so far as to say it's the responsible thing to do. Yesterday, Limbaugh was back on the air and was claiming that he was not in favor of secession, and that he was only quoting unnamed bloggers. I listened to that broadcast and while he did not say he agreed with them, he did say this, in response to a question about ever winning elections again from a caller and his producer Bo Snerdley:[62]

I thought you were asking me something else when you said, "Can we win?" I thought you meant can we win the culture, can we dominate the culture. **I actually think -- and I've referenced this, I've alluded to this a couple of times cause I've seen others allude to this. I actually think that we're trending toward secession.** *I see more and more people asking what in the world do we have in common with the people who live in, say, New York? What is there that makes us believe that there is enough of us there to even have a chance at winning New York, especially if you're talking about votes.*

I see a lot of bloggers -- I can't think of names right now -- a lot of bloggers have written extensively about how distant and separated and how much more separated our culture is becoming politically and that it can't go on this way. There cannot be a peaceful coexistence of two completely different theories of life, theories of government, theories of how we manage our affairs. We can't be in this dire a conflict without something giving somewhere along the way.

---

62 https://www.rushlimbaugh.com/daily/2020/12/09/i-still-havent-given-up-on-the-idea-that-we-can-win-back-the-culture/

I know that there's a sizable and growing sentiment for people who believe that that is where we're headed whether we want to or not. Whether we want to go there or not. I myself haven't made up my mind. I still haven't given up the idea that we are the majority and that all we have to do is find a way to unite and win. **And our problem is the fact that there are just so many RINOs, so many Republicans in the Washington establishment who will do anything to maintain their membership in the establishment because of the perks and the opportunities that are presented for their kids and so forth.**

The bloggers he was alluding to are more than likely from American Thinker, American Greatness and Frontpage Mag, plus a heaping helping of some of the folks right here at the HQ. In any case, the reason the Left went nuts about this is because all they heard was "secession" uttered by Rush Limbaugh. The fatal mistake they've been making for 32 years is thinking Rush Limbaugh brainwashes millions of people into thinking what he thinks, when in reality, Rush Limbaugh is merely giving voice to what millions of people are already thinking. My own perception is, while he certainly did not openly call for a split, his tone taken in context with everything else he was saying seemed as if he did not object to it, much that he did not want it to come about. I wouldn't want it, but if your leg is gangrenous, at a certain point it's got to go. I'll go back and re-listen to the segment just to see if my perception is correct.

Regardless, secession, national divorce, dissolution, whatever you want to call it is in the public conscious. The Enemy does not want it because they want to dominate, control and punish us for being everything they are not - righteous, moral, hardworking, successful, G-d fearing, truly compassionate and most of all, independent. It's the same rationale behind the Muslim world's utter hatred of the state of Israel and why they want its destruction. Israel's existence, and its absolute success as a free and open society stands in sharp contrast to the misery, squalor, failure and despair of every nation around it. If ever America were split in two, our nation would become a Trumpist Americanist superpower while the Leftist nation would devolve into a hell on Earth to rival Venezuela, Haiti, Cuba and Zimbabwe. It would be a negation of everything that they believe in, and so, it must not be allowed to exist. Again, in their twisted weltanschauung, it (that is WE) is the embodiment of evil and must either be subjugated or destroyed. It's the same old story; lather, rinse, repeat until paradise on Earth is achieved, no matter how many millions of lives are ground into dust.

And that brings us to the other part of Rush's comments that I highlighted as it now pertains to the President's ultimate gambit in restoring his victory for a second term; the fact that his fate is in the hands of a political party that is worse than dead. It's the undead zombie accomplice of the Enemy. With such stalwart leadership as Mitch McConnell congratulating

- CONGRATULATING - Joe Biden and Kamala Harris, and praising the former to high heaven for all his years of service in the Senate.[63] The fucking gall.

But wait, there's more! Arguably one of the worst human beings on the planet, Mitt "Pee-Air Defecto" Romney is demanding we give up and get behind the Polident-Elect, while at the same time bemoaning that Trumpism is here to stay.[64]

Yup, I'm just filled with strength and confidence that the GOP is going to recognize the alternate slate of electors and then vote 30-20 in the House to elect Trump. Sheesh. As an aside, Rush Limbaugh is kind of a metaphor for America. Real America. Stricken as he is with cancer, his situation very much in doubt, he still somehow manages to pull himself together and fight.

Well, be it Limbaugh or the nation, in spite of everything, miracles do happen. Until noon on January 20th, I'll endeavor to persevere... and keep the Zippo away from my thinning pate.

Thursday, December 17, 2020

The big story is the impending report from DNI John Ratcliffe as well as its implications for President Trump's final gambit - Congressional Republicans discarding the Democrat electors in the six swing states (plus New Mexico),

---

63 https://www.cnsnews.com/article/washington/cnsnewscom-staff/senate-majority-leader-mitch-mcconnell-electoral-college-has

64 https://newsthud.com/romney-calls-for-strong-trump-supporters-in-gop-to-speak-out-and-get-behind-biden/

recognizing the GOP alternates and thereby voting to restore his legitimate victory for another term. On the downside, there are a few moving parts for this whole thing to be put in motion, with the biggest problem being the human element. Either out of hatred for Trump and the desire to restore the Deep State status quo, fear of political and actual physical retribution or both, the collective backbone of several hundred Republicans is in serious doubt. Now that said, much like the womp rat-width exhaust port on the Death Star, it may be a one-in-a-million shot to vaporize it but as of right now it is a shot.

Perhaps that's why Mitch the surrender turtle[65] shit his pants yesterday, flapping his goiterous turkey wattle that the party collectively recognize the Electoral College's decision and become accessories after the fact to the greatest crime in American history. From what I understand, all it takes is one Congressman and one Senator to object to the EC to start the procedural ball rolling, and we have over a hundred of the former and probably a good half dozen or so of the latter eager to tell Mitch to blow it out his Chinese finger trap.

Meanwhile, getting back to DNI Ratcliffe's report, it should be noted that it only covers one aspect of the election theft, that of foreign interference. No, not Russia buying $150,000 worth of anti-Hillary Facebook ads in 2016 but a coordinated effort involving China, Iran, Venezuela and perhaps Russia, and the compromised and rigged Dominion voting machines among other things. That alone should be

---

65 Mitch McConnell

enough to pull the emergency brake on the crazy train and reverse our headlong plunge into the abyss. The fly in the ointment, as has been the case for the past four years, is a Trump ally at the top of an agency relying on hundreds or even thousands of his underlings that in whole or part are firmly in the enemy camp and have been sabotaging this administration since day one. Given the proven infiltration of the Communist Chinese into our government, bureaucracies, as well as the proven bribery of some of our highest elected officials and their family members of same, the Ratcliffe report if done honestly would certainly implicate CIA, FBI, DoJ and a litany of other alphabet soup agencies that were supposed to secure our election systems from foreign interference. In the event, they more than likely aided and abetted it in 2020 if not 2016 and who knows how many other prior elections.

Additionally, we have this nugget from money honey Maria Bartiromo:[66]

> "An intel source told me President Trump did, in fact, win the election. He says that it is up to the Supreme Court to hear suits from other cases across the country to stop the clock. This follows the high court's refusal to hear the lawsuit from Texas Attorney General Ken Paxton."

---

66 https://www.americanthinker.com/blog/2020/12/maria_bartiromo_drops_the_mother_of_all_bombshells.html

While all of us were ripping the Court over its refusal to hear that case because of standing issues, is it possible that they ditched it in order to get to the individual state suits? Honestly, at this point, who the hell knows or even cares. As per usual, we follow the rules while the Enemy does anything and everything to accrue and hold on to power. And that's giving the Court completely undeserved credit for being above the board and impartial in this. The steal is real. It happened. The evidence of all kinds is massive and incontestable. The six state legislatures should never have certified their votes and at a minimum not awarded any electors to the College. But they did. Texas' lawsuit should have at a minimum been heard and by all rights SCOUTS should've sided with the plaintiff and thrown out the fraudulent results. Yet here we are. We'll see what happens with Bartiromo's source vis a vis SCOTUS, but I'm not holding my breath.

Not to be defeatist, but we are going to have to prepare for the possibility of America as founded ceasing to exist at noon on January 20th, 2021. The question is, upwards of 200 million of us will essentially become dissidents in our own country, internally exiled like Andrei Sakharov and Natan Scharansky. So, as Christopher Roach at American Greatness ponders, what comes next?[67]

The most workable model is less Ronald Reagan's GOP and something more like Poland's Solidarity movement in the 1980s. Even under Communism

---

67 https://amgreatness.com/2020/12/16/what-is-to-be-done

and the imposition of martial law, this grassroots trade union managed to resist the regime and convert the government's suppression into a high cost in international censure. Some of Solidarity's more important tactics included underground schools and workers' strikes.

What if we went on strike?

It is difficult to adjust to the reality that ordinary politics essentially are over. The signs of a slow-motion breakdown of the old system first appeared only as fragments: Supreme Court cases on controversial social questions, sustained government growth under both Republican and Democratic administrations, intelligence agencies meddling in an election, and the full-bore resistance by the bureaucracy to the Trump Administration. The real "mask off" moment has been the suspect election of 2020.

We have to face reality and fight the good fight effectively on the terrain on which we now find ourselves. That means changing our lifestyles and efforts in ways that achieve maximum personal independence, mutual support, and tangible results.

There is quite a good essay on the conditions in Chile that led to General Augusto Pinochet from Jay Schalin over at American Thinker. He concludes:[68]

> *The Chilean coup of 1973 offers hard lessons that many will not accept because these lessons do not appeal to superficial norms of fairness and tolerance. For one, electoral politics do not always equate to human flourishing but can instead bring repression. For another,* **a nation must deal harshly with those who would deny liberty to the rest.**

Of course, Pinochet had the entire armed forces and police of Chile behind him. We do not have that, not in its entirety. But I can dream, can't I?

Friday, December 18, 2020

Yesterday afternoon, Weasel Zippers teased a Tweet from Heshmat Alavi, a journalist who covers the Iranian dissident and Middle East beats wherein he reported that CBS' Catherine Herridge was reporting that Ratcliffe told the network his report concludes that there was indeed interference in the 2020 election from China, Iran and Russia.[69] That's kind of a big effin' deal as Polident-Elect Mushmouth[70]

---

68 https://www.americanthinker.com/articles/2020/12/rethinking_pinochet_in_praise_of_strength.html

69 https://www.weaselzippers.us/461030-breaking-catherine-herridge-of-cbs-director-of-national-intelligence-confirms-china-interference-in-election/

70 President-Elect Joe Biden

might say, but since then, I have seen nothing else either in the usual dreck propaganda channels or from real journalists in the blogosphere. In any case, today is the day that his report is supposed to drop so before I wet myself with excitement, the niggling suspicion is still there that, like Jimmy "PineSol" Comey did four years ago, a litany of charges will be read off but the conclusion will be that the interference had no effect on changing the outcome of the election. Yeah, I know. I'm too young to be such a hard-bitten cynic. On the plus side, Ratcliffe is supposedly an ally of the President but, as has been the case for the past four years, the embedded, untouchables in every agency and department in the DC bureaucracy will work to sabotage any effort to advance the Trump agenda. Certainly Ratcliffe will have had to contend with this, especially with the CIA, DoJ, FBI, DIA and the other intel and LE agencies that are actually in bed - like Swalwell quite literally - with our enemies. Anyway, it'll be what it'll be, so stay tuned.

Meanwhile, in the Hail Mary department, some encouraging news broke late yesterday, in that freshman Senator Tommy Tuberville has indicated that he is strongly considering joining the House Republicans in objecting to the Electoral College votes come January 6th. In the House, fellow Alabamian Mo Brooks has gathered 18 colleagues to sign a letter calling for hearings before the January 6th deadline wherein Congress would certify the EC vote and clear the way for the fraud to be signed, sealed and delivered. No way Malig-Nancy Pelosi agrees to that but be that as it may, all it takes in either chamber is just one individual to object to the certification, which then would trigger debate and, well, you know the rest.

As I said, it's a Hail Mary not from the Jimmy Hoffa end 100 yards to the other end of Giants Stadium but from the Santa Monica Pier, if not the M-79 star system. But, it's still a chance. Why else would walking goiter Mitch McConnell plead with GOP Senators not to do this? The raison d'etre from the talking head propagandists that it would lead to a wipeout in both Georgia Senate seat runoffs is idiotic. If anything, if Perdue and Loeffler actually went on the offensive, it would rally the troops. While shambling shit-heel Chris "Krispy Kreosote" Christie warning the GOP not to oppose the Electoral College results and that "Biden clearly won" is repulsive but it is illuminating. Same thing with the hard-on-with-the-chemically-induced-hard-on Bob Dole, who also hurled invective at our President for not surrendering.

I said yesterday that this was the President's final gambit but I was mistaken. There is one final option for him if this fails and it's nuclear, metaphorically but almost literally - the invocation of the Insurrection Act.

As recently as two weeks ago, before the Supreme Court sided with our enemies and ignored the Constitution in denying the clear standing of Texas et al to sue the rogue states, Lieutenant General Tom McInerney (Ret.) declared we're in the most "dangerous situation since the Civil War." He went on to say "When you coordinate six to ten states, using cyber warfare, to change the outcome of the election in favor of whoever you want, these are treasonous acts." He called for the President to invoke the Insurrection Act.[71]

Obviously, all hell would break loose if President Trump were to do this. The consequences of allowing this to happen would be far, far worse; in effect, the complete surrender of our nation to our enemies, foreign and domestic with all of the horror that that entails.

We talked about the actions of Augusto Pinochet in saving Chile from turning into the hell on earth that is Cuba, Venezuela, and Zimbabwe, among others, today. But Pinochet had the entire military and police forces of Chile firmly behind him. Considering individuals like James Mattis, William McRaven, Stanley McChrystal - who orchestrated the fomenting of so-called "orange revolutions" overseas and is directly linked to doing the same thing here in the wake of what happened 6 weeks ago - among others, that situation is in doubt. At least on the flag officer level. It would be interesting to hear what General McInerney has to say on this. Tinfoil hat on: If he is indeed an ally and not just saying this to get Trump to do something that would have him arrested (tinfoil hat off), I wonder if he knows that the troops are with him.

I know that after every legal and procedural avenue has been all but exhausted - as a result of corruption and complicity by those with the power and duty to stop this - at least 80 million Americans will stand with this President if he is forced to, shall we say, pull the trigger. I will also say

---

71 https://www.brighteon.com/7497ff5e-44b3-44d4-9363-c9fcbea100ba

that having to do this is probably a half-step below that of ordering a nuclear attack on another nation. But with the nation and indeed the world on a knife edge of catastrophe, his duty is crystal clear. Everyone else has abrogated their oaths out of fear, greed, complicity or some combination of those.

While we still have one chance left of averting disaster with the Senate and House Republicans stepping up and doing their duty, if that fails, this President must do his duty.

Thursday, December 24, 2020

Along with the continued fallout over the President's ripping the 5,500 page looting of the Treasury disguised as a Chinese COVID relief bill and his counter-offer (hopefully as a stand-alone bill that shreds the other 5,499-ish pages), we have news this morning that Trump has pardoned another 26 individuals including Democrat/Deep State persecuted political prisoners Paul Manafort and Roger Stone. It never ceases to amaze and infuriate me how the Left manages to portray itself as noble, moral and just no matter how obvious their fraud, how egregious their crimes, or how massive the evidence of their failures and guilt. I expect vermin like Paypal Jayapal and Titty Caca AOC (who may very well find herself back at a bar [if they ever open again] due to New York losing a congressional district) to open the flapping exhaust pipes above their chins to spout their bile. But then there's Ben

Sasse-hole. I don't think I ever saw a faster costume change than this douchebag. Touted as the cream of the crop of the next generation of young conservatives, it took him about a nanosecond to get on his knees to suckle the length and breadth of K-Street and the Chamber of Commerce. How Nebraskans fell for this cheap punk I'll never know. I'd say he should be primaried but considering the legitimacy of our elections going forward, we're probably stuck with this jagoff for the next half-century or so. If we still exist. If G-d is good, I'll me moldering in my grave well before that and not have to endure that particularly noxious vat of acridity.

Speaking of rigged elections, White House advisor Peter Navarro has written a comprehensive report that goes into great detail on specifically how the 2020 election was stolen. For anyone claiming there's no evidence, it's all speculation and conspiracy theories, etc. etc., Navarro really lays it out.[72]

> *This is election fraud at the retail level. Voting illegally, or voting twice, or in multiple states, is a felony. These allegations are easy to verify -- but so far, no court has allowed the Trump team to provide the lists of voters Navarro cites. And states controlled by Democrats have systematically refused any outside examination of their voter rolls and screamed "voter suppression" whenever groups such as Judicial Watch have forced them to hand over the evidence in the courts.*

---

72 https://www.americanthinker.com/articles/2020/12/why_democrats_should_read_the_navarro_report.html

Then you have the cemetery vote -- at least 8,000 of them in Pennsylvania, and probably more in Philadelphia, Milwaukee, and Detroit -- and "ghost" voters who were added to the voter rolls on Election Day by poll workers. In Michigan, for example, thousands of people who showed up without ID were assigned birth dates in 1900 and allowed to vote. This is fraud organized and carried out by others.

In addition, Navarro describes multiple cases of wholesale fraud, especially in Wisconsin and Michigan, where election workers were caught on camera or by multiple eyewitnesses who submitted sworn affidavits running batches of ballots repeatedly through tabulating machines. "Evidence of these particular kinds of "ballot stuffing" are present across all six battleground states," Navarro notes.

It's a must read, unless you're a Democrat or Ben Sassehole, but I repeat myself. In any case, Eric Croomer the security director of Dominion is suing Sidney Powell, Lin Wood and Trump Campaign. Well, discovery should be lit. Bring it on...

...Lastly, in his final broadcast for the year, Rush Limbaugh was particularly open and honest about his health. For long time listeners, he does take this opportunity to thank his audience but all things considered, many people sensed something a bit deeper and more urgent in his words and his tone. Diagnosed almost exactly a year ago with stage four lung cancer, he admitted that his doctors did not think he'd make it into the fall. That he is still here is a miracle. I hope and pray yesterday was not his last broadcast, and that he is with us for many more years to come.

Monday, December 28, 2020

Right now, the final cards in the fight to restore his victory are set to be played either in the SCOTUS, Congress or some combination of both. Or, as the first link in that section suggests in the mind and heart of perhaps a lone individual who could change history:[73]

> *The central point is that the VP, as the presiding officer and final authority, has the unquestionable authority to declare that the states in question have not conducted presidential elections. There will be wailing and gnashing of teeth, but no one has the authority to override his decision.*

> *The statement says nothing about who might or might not have "won" the contested states. Rather, by not following their own laws, as enacted by their own legislatures, they have violated Article II, Section 1. Thus, they have not conducted an election, and their results are void.*

---

73 https://www.americanthinker.com/articles/2020/12/its_for_mike_pence_to_judge_whether_a_presidential_election_was_held_at_all.html

If the votes of all seven contested states are registered as zero, President Trump will have 232 votes, and Joe Biden will have 222. The 12th Amendment says, "[T]he votes shall then be counted[.] ... The person having the greatest number of votes for President, shall be the President[.]"

In plain language, Donald Trump will be re-elected, since he has a majority of the actual electoral votes. There will be no need to involve the House of Representatives to resolve a contingent election.

Richard Nixon chose not to contest the 1960 election because he felt that winning that way would lead to an ungovernable country. If V.P. Pence does this, that same argument might be made. But is the country governable even now? *Blue states such as California, Oregon, Washington, New York, New Jersey, and Michigan are already operating in an openly lawless manner with their "emergency" "COVID-related" restrictions. Their denial of the civil rights of law-abiding citizens is horrific. Their refusal to do basic policing and law enforcement is a recipe for open war.* ***How much worse would things be if the V.P. lived up to his oath and upheld the law?***

Those bits that I emphasized underscore what I and many of us have been stating in one way or another for years now. Trying to fight what is a lawless internal enemy by doing things under the rubric of "regular order" or being afraid of setting a dangerous precedent by going outside regular order is like watching your entire neighborhood go up in flames while trying to save your house by peeing on the lawn.

Only a fool living in denial cannot see that there's no going back to "normal" for whatever definition of normal there might be. If indeed Mike Pence can do what the article states, he cannot afford to play it safe. From what I have seen and heard of him these past four years, I like. He's affable, level-headed and by all accounts seems to be a decent, G-d fearing man. That said, he is a lifelong politician and in many ways has been molded by DC - the entity that is his boss' nemesis. Pence's caving on RFRA did not inspire strength and confidence. The question is, if indeed he does have the power, does he understand the consequences of not fulfilling his oath and doing his duty?

As bad as the chaos and violence of restoring President Trump's stolen victory may be in the short term, allowing the theft of the 2020 election will condemn our nation, society and way of life too death, along with much of the rest of world.

Tuesday, December 29, 2020

Louie "Go-Go" Gohmert filed a lawsuit at, or against, VP Mike Pence that instructs him to do his constitutional duty in using his plenary power to reject the Biden electors from the six disputed states and install the Trump slate.[74]

> *"The 2020 presidential election was one we'd expect to see in a banana republic, not the United States of America. In fact, the rampant fraud and unconstitutional actions that took place were so egregious that seven contested states -- Arizona, Georgia, Michigan, New Mexico, Nevada, Pennsylvania, and Wisconsin all sent dueling slates of electors to Congress,"* Gohmert said in a statement.

> *"This puts Vice President Mike Pence in a position where some argue he has to choose between morality and the law. That is not the case,"* Gohmert continued.

The author of the essay I linked yesterday was unequivocal in his declaration that Pence already has the authority to do what Gohmert's suit is forcing him to do. Considering he, Gohmert, was a judge and someone who has more than a passing knowledge of the Constitution and electoral procedures, I'm not sure I get what this is all about. Perhaps it's a pre-emptive move to give the VP legal cover. In any case, given the state of our judiciary, and the fact that January 6th is only eight days away, it seems to reek of desperation.

That said, it certainly looks as if we have a least one Senator and one Representative who are going to object to recognizing the results from the Electoral College, so that is

---

74 https://dailycaller.com/2020/12/28/louie-gohmert-republicans-sue-mike-pence-over-turn-presidential-election-biden-kelli-ward/

going to trigger a debate. Yet given the nature of the GOP, the outcome of that is certainly not a lead pipe cinch. Far from it. So, like yesterday, Mike Pence - seemingly - holds the fate of this nation in his hands.

Then again, maybe not.[75]

As of yet, there has been no storm, no Kraken. Trump has followed the Constitution, making legal arguments up to and including the U.S. Supreme Court. What Vice President Pence does when it is time to again follow the Constitution and certify the Electoral College votes is to be determined.

Will a massive declassification of criminal and seditious activities subdue the Democrats? Will Trump win without a bloody battle? Time will tell.

At this point, it's a binary choice. Either Trump is in over his head and will be dragged out of office. Or he is executing his plan, on his terms and timing, as he has done since his famous escalator ride at Trump Tower in 2015.

Trump knows the stakes for himself, his family, and America if Kamala Harris and Joe Biden get the keys to the kingdom and promptly hand them over

---

75 https://www.americanthinker.com/articles/2020/12/is_nothing_happening_or_is_trump_is_channeling_sun_tzu.html

to China. Want to bet against Trump? How has that worked out in the past?...

...Is Trump unprepared? Au contraire. Listen to Oprah interviewing him in 1988,[76] more than 30 years ago. He looks younger but sounds the same as he does now, speaking of China, immigration, and electoral politics. Trump has been preparing for this moment most of his adult life.

Buckle up for an interesting few weeks ahead.

You can say that again.

Wednesday, December 30, 2020

If Joe-Blow77 is/are installed and the Georgia Senate seats are also stolen (as I fear is a likely scenario), Section 230 protection for the Enemy Propaganda Complex will be reinstated as if it never went away in the first place. All this talk about 2022 and 2024 is as idiotic as the illusion of regular order, parliamentary procedure, comity and all that other rot. I mean, for fuck's sake; the judge in Georgia who blocked the purging of voter rolls in two counties is the sister of Tank Abrams.[78][79] The litany of corruption in that state as well as

---

76 https://www.youtube.com/watch?v=GZpMJeynBeg

77 Joe Biden-Kamala Harris

78 https://newsthud.com/judge-who-is-the-sister-of-stacey-abrams-blocks-voter-roll-purge-in-2-georgia-counties/

79 Stacey Abrams

the five others is well documented and shows beyond any reasonable doubt that the 2020 election was indeed stolen. John Lott, who is the nation's foremost expert on gun crimes, 2A issues and an adviser to the DOJ just released a report that concludes up to 368,000 "excess votes" did indeed tip the scales for[80] the Polident-Elect[81] in the critical swing states:

> *"Increased fraud can take many forms: higher rates of filling out absentee ballots for people who hadn't voted, dead people voting, ineligible people voting, or even payments to legally registered people for their votes. [...] The estimates here indicate that there were 70,000 to 79,000 "excess" votes in Georgia and Pennsylvania. Adding Arizona, Michigan, Nevada, and Wisconsin, the total increases to up to 289,000 excess votes," the summary notes.*

> *Lott, who now serves as a Senior Adviser for Research and Statistics at the Office of Justice Programs, also adds that there are two reasons to even believe the aforementioned numbers are "underestimates":*

>> 1) the estimates using precinct level data assume that there is no fraud occurring with in-person voting and, 2) the voter turnout estimates do not account for ballots for the

---

80 https://newsthud.com/judge-who-is-the-sister-of-stacey-abrams-blocks-voter-roll-purge-in-2-georgia-counties/

81 President-Elect Joe Biden

opposing candidate that are lost, destroyed, or replaced with ballots filled out for the other candidate.

Lott points to universal mail-in voting as a hotbed for fraud, remarking "unsecured absentee ballots create the potential that either fraudulent ballots will be introduced or votes to be destroyed."

This is on top of what we all saw happen in real time on election night, when the observers were kicked out of the tabulating centers, the doors and windows sealed and the pallets of ballots trucked in and, voila! As if the GOP state legislators and officials, did not see this coming. They did and yet still certified the electoral votes. Considering the character of most Republicans in the House and especially in the Senate mirrors that of the useless, spineless, corrupted jellyfish in the state legislatures in question, I am dreading next Wednesday like the plague (a real one, not the phony one foisted on us by the Chi-Coms and their Leftist agents in our own borders).

And for the third day in a row, all eyes turn to Vice President Pence. Edward Davis over at American Thinker argues that the GOPers in Congress should not contest the electors and leave the heavy lifting to the veep:[82]

---

82 https://www.americanthinker.com/blog/2020/12/gop_congressional_challenges_to_
electors_would_be_a_catastrophic_tactical_mistake.html

...opinion has long been divided on what the vice president is empowered to do in his vote-counting role. Ivan Raiklin is hardly alone in his argument. It should not surprise us. Constitutional law frequently is not black and white, as seen in the numerous 5-4 Supreme Court decisions by Justices applying the same law to the same facts.

In other words, Pence should go for it. He need only interpret "votes" as votes from states not in dispute, and count them accordingly. He could declare, "I will not count the Biden electors, or the competing slates of Trump electors, in disputed states where there is overwhelming credible evidence of systemic fraud." Thus would he restore the election win to President Trump, from whom it was audaciously stolen.

What would Pence have to lose? A commenter at Legal Insurrection observed:

> Pence should refuse to count votes from the contested states, and dare someone to sue him in court. Then the SCOTUS can simply docket that for January 21, 2021. If the SCOTUS can't stop states from stealing elections, they damn well don't have the power to stop Pence from counting the votes any way he wants to.

One caveat: This has been a season in which everyone seems to be letting us down. Why expect Pence to be any different? The Washington Post reported, "Pence is hoping for a low-key Jan. 6 and is not planning any unnecessary drama, aides said, intending to stick to his perfunctory role. He is eyeing a trip overseas soon after."

But the Post report might be inaccurate, or this could be Trump disinformation intended to cause the opposition to let down their guard.

As for the mention of no "unnecessary drama" in Pence's plans, that doesn't rule out necessary drama. **The Democratic election theft was bold and shocking. It calls for a bold, shocking correction.**

As I have often stated, the more dire the situation, the more unassailable the logic, the more massive the evidence, the more clear the remedy, the more you can count on any given Republican to ignore it all and do exactly the wrong thing. So, the $62 trillion dollar question is, is Mike Pence any given Republican? With a nod towards the great Milton Friedman PBUH, will the weight of history compel the wrong man (or at best perhaps the unlikely man) to do the right thing?

The world wonders...

Thursday, December 31, 2020

New Year's Eve. Normally this is a time of promise for new beginnings and hope, but given what we've been through and what we've experienced, I'm dreading what lies ahead. It's hard to believe that less than a year ago, our economy was booming, China, Iran and their surrogates in this country, the Democrat Party were either on the ropes or reeling, as President Trump was well on the way to a massive re-election victory. If I've learned anything over the past four years is that given the evil that exists in this world, nothing is ever safe, certain or secure, not only on a cosmological level but for sure on a political level. With a nod to Sinclair Lewis, it certainly can happen here because starting in 2020 it did happen here.

Despite the cover of a manufactured phony health crisis to subvert an already compromised electoral process, President Donald J. Trump was well on his way to beating even that massive cheat and securing at least a 400-electoral vote and popular vote landslide. That is, until a water pipe in Atlanta caused an in-your-face deluge -- of fake ballots dumped in four major metropolitan areas across six states, drowning not just the real votes, but the Constitution with it.

I didn't think the nation could have sunk any lower than the attempt to overthrow the 2016 election via the Russia collusion hoax. The undeniable exposure of people entrusted with enforcing our laws and protecting our national security as cheap crooks, drunk on power and their own narcissistic delusions of elitism was shocking in the extreme. A lot of folks took that as a sign that Trump and the nation itself were in real danger. I made the mistake of thinking surviving it meant the firewalls were secure. I don't think I could have been more wrong about anything else in my life. I will not make that mistake again.

And yet, here I am once again talking about January 6th. Am I friggin' stupid or what?! I just wasted pixels as well as my time (hopefully not yours), burnishing my newly won credentials in the He-Man Hard-Bitten Cynics Club, and now I'm going to go on about the GOPers in Congress or VP Pence delivering us from Old Sparky with a last minute reprieve. We all know that whether fearing for their lives, or worse, as part of the institutional corruption that Donald J. Trump was elected - TWICE - to eradicate, the majority of Republicans at the local, state and federal level cannot or will not uphold their oaths to defend the Constitution.

But what sustains me is that in spite of all that, there are men and women who still have a conscience to do the moral, legal and righteous thing by saving the nation from being extinguished. So far it's Josh Hawley in the Senate as well as several Congressmen in the House. Rush Limbaugh discussed the nuts and bolts of the process last week and they are hyperlinked here if you're curious.[83] Whether they ulti-mately succeed - please G-d - is neither the issue nor the reason for my hope. It's because, few in number though they

83 https://www.rushlimbaugh.com/daily/2020/12/16/the-turtle-is-determined-to-stop-the-one-long-shot-scenario-left-for-trump/

may be, they are there. And while few in number on Capitol Hill, there are tens of millions of like-minded citizens just like them across the country. The last person that I ever expected to lead a movement with the goal of national revival was Donald Trump. The Enemy makes the fatal error of thinking that Trump was a one-off, or like Rush Limbaugh, Trump brainwashed "bitter-clinger" "deplorables" into voting for him. The truth which deep down the Enemy[84] must know is that those two men, titans of communication and influence though they may be only reflect the mood of the people.

The brazenness that the Enemy shows in its actions against the American people is in direct proportion with which the American people have rejected and continue to reject them. And for the capital crime of rejecting them in 2016, we have been sentenced to death. With the bureaucracy, the courts, the media and the schools arrayed against us, our only way of fighting back was every two to four years was at the ballot box. As of eight weeks ago, that is now gone forever, so forget 2022 or 2024 and quite probably beyond that. Whether Trump remains or is forced out, we are still here.

If you thought 2020 was bad, you ain't seen nothing yet. Things are going to get a lot worse, and it's going to get personal. But where there is life, there is hope. Don't vest all your trust in one man, be it Trump, Rush or whoever. First and foremost, you have to put your trust in yourself. Man up, woman up. We all have responsibilities that keep us occupied

---

84 The Democrat, Media, Deep State Complex

with putting food on the table and a roof over the heads of our loved ones. But what is all of that worth if the freedom to live your life as you see fit, or to try to make it better for your progeny, is denied you? A moment of truth is fast approaching. I can't tell you what to do because I myself don't know what to do. That's what's so frustrating and depressing.

One thing is clear. We cannot go on as before and while the Enemy has a stranglehold on us we certainly will not go on as before because things are going to be on their terms. But no one is infallible. Not even them. As we reflect back on this past year and the three prior to that, the verdict from my perspective is in: President Trump will go down as one of the greatest presidents in our history. In spite of all the political and social forces arrayed against him, he instituted the greatest economic boom in history, engineered major foreign policy triumphs by challenging geopolitical rivals and enemies and orchestrating Middle East peace deals thought impossible, and helped bring about vaccines against a Chinese engineered biological weapon at "warp speed," among other things.

But his greatest achievement is exposing the decades-long generational corruption of our government to a vast swathe of the populace, heretofore unaware or uncaring. To put an ironic twist on a disgusting threat from an equally disgusting woman who once was first lady, what President Trump revealed will never allow us to be able to go on with our lives as before. And ultimately, that is a good thing.

Friday, January 1, 2021

In the House, upwards of 140 Republicans are going to vote to object to the results, including all representatives from Pennsylvania who will contest their state's electors. I assume they will also contest the electors from the other stolen states? And what about the 56 other Republican congressmen? Meanwhile, over in the Senate, the situation is in serious doubt despite Josh Hawley announcing his intention to object. The hatred of President Trump among many Senate Republicans, be it driven by petty personal jealousy or the fact that he remains the greatest existential threat to their being in on their graft as part of the dismantling of America as founded, has probably doomed the effort to failure. Does anyone really think that the Lord in Heaven is going to suddenly miracle the collective ass of Romney or Murkowski or Collins with morality, honor and ethics? Pat Toomey - Pat friggin' Toomey, whose own state is at the epicenter of executive and judicial malfeasance as well as massive on-scene, in your face ballot dumping and spoliation of evidence after the fact - says about Hawley's planned objection, that "he strongly disagrees." Check that; Toomey had one of his flunkies make the statement to a hack from Politico: "Senator Toomey made his views on Senator Hawley's planned objection clear. He strongly disagrees." How very brave.

I have developed a sort of theorem about these things. No matter how blatant the crime or situation and how clear-cut the remedy, those allegedly on our side will not fail to either do nothing or the exact wrong thing to let it slide, carve it in stone and make it worse. While it is heartening that we do have people in government like Josh Hawley willing to put whatever political aspirations he might have on the line to take a stand, especially when the chips are really down, sadly he is an outlier at least in terms of the makeup of Congress as well as state governments across the nation. The question is, is he a harbinger of things to come or the last vestige of a dying breed? The same can of course be asked of President Trump.

The corruption of our government, which is of course downstream of society in general, is so thorough and has been going on for so long that the brazenness and even eagerness to openly steal a national election was perhaps inevitable. Same with the nearly three-year attempt to overthrow the 2016 election results, which when it fizzled drove Enemy to use the pretext of a supposed health crisis (or consort with Communist China to bring the virus here in the first place as a stage-setter) to destroy the already flimsy firewalls that protect electoral integrity. And even then, when that failed, the halting of the count and the trucking in of the pallets of ballots.

As for the actions of Vice President Pence come next Wednesday, Legal Insurrection's William Jacobson, has a nice bucket of ice water:[85]

---

85 https://legalinsurrection.com/2020/12/january-6-no-mike-pence-cant-just-reject-electoral-certifications/

A claim has circulated widely in the past few days that Vice President Mike Pence, as President of the Senate, has the power and discretion to reject certifications. If Pence had such power and chose to exercise it, it would be over, but he doesn't.

Here is the relevant language of Article II, Section I (after the 12th Amendment)(emphasis added):

> The Electors shall meet in their respective States, and vote by Ballot for two Persons, of whom one at least shall not be an Inhabitant of the same State with themselves. And they shall make a List of all the Persons voted for, and of the Number of Votes for each; which List they shall sign and certify, and transmit sealed to the Seat of the Government of the United States, directed to the President of the Senate. The President of the Senate shall, in the Presence of the Senate and House of Representatives, open all the Certificates, and the Votes shall then be counted...

...I've gone farther down this rabbit hole than I should have, particularly on New Year's Eve. If you want "to fight" on January 6 for political reasons, I get it, I'm as frustrated as you are (maybe more so).

It's just bothered me that really bad legal takes -- and
these are not the first -- have mislead well-meaning
and justifiably-concerned people to think the outcome
on January 6 is going to be different.

Jacobson goes into quite a bit of detail on prior cases involving the 12th amendment. He's also no slouch when it comes to constitutional law either. He also goes on to mention Go-Go Gohmert's[86] suit against Pence stating that the VP has countersued stating he's not the proper party and that relief must come from Congress.

I don't mean to be a downer but the situation is what it is. It's kind of a miracle that Obama and company, who did incredible damage to this nation politically, economically and socially, still failed to deliver the fatal blow and in many ways set the stage for President Trump. Actually, Obama was helped quite a bit by Clinton and both Bushes and to be fair, Nixon and Ford, but I digress. In any case, when the Enemy controlled both houses of Congress and the Oval Office, they could have easily given amnesty to the tens of millions of illegal aliens already in country - which Dubya almost succeeded in doing in his last year in office, the bastard - and it would've been lights out America right there, as Texas and perhaps Florida would've gone blue. Those who are pulling the strings of Joe+Blow are not going to make that mistake again. And even if they did, does anyone really think that any election from now on is not going to either be pre-rigged or stolen after the fact?

86 Rep. Louie Gohmert

I have no idea what is going to happen next Wednesday, nor 20 days from now. All I can say is we cannot know the future with any degree of certainty. To be sure, the Enemy holds the high ground and perhaps all of the cards. But they are not infallible. And we are still going to be here. In the millions. Let's hope the common emotion is anger and not resignation.

Monday, January 4, 2021

It's Year Zero. We continue to be in lockdown limbo as well as a state of either national dissolution or subjugation thanks to the theft of the 2020 election as well as the quite probable theft of the two Georgia senate seats after tomorrow that will seal the fate of the American experiment.

And yet the day after tomorrow, Congress will convene to vote to certify the results of the Electoral College. Barring President Trump invoking the Insurrection Act, declaring martial law or going full Pinochet, Wednesday is likely the final gambit to try and stave off disaster, and restore his legitimate victory. On a positive note, both Mo Brooks in the House, now supported (surprisingly) by Minority Leader Kevin McCarthy along with Josh Hawley and Ted Cruz in the Senate have openly stated that they and a not insignificant number of their colleagues in each chamber will be challenging the results, specifically in the six states where blatant provable fraud, before, during and after Election Day occurred. On the downside, the fact that every single

Republican from both chambers is not fully on board with this effort is disappointing, to say the least, if not revelatory.

Obviously, crooked flim-flam artists like Romney, Murkowski, Collins, Thune, Sasse and others were always going to make this effort a 1,000-to-1 shot. The most galling thing about them, as well as the Enemy, is their claiming of the moral high ground, and invoking everything from the Constitution, The Bible and Jesus Christ, and "the will of the people" all while doing everything they can to snuff them all out in their quest for absolute power. But it's particularly painful when someone whom you thought was on your side joins in with the others and delivers a swift rhetorical kick in the yarbles.[87]

Sen. Tom Cotton (R-AR) became the first Republican senator on Sunday night who is actually a supporter of President Donald Trump's agenda to oppose a challenge of the electoral college, issuing a statement saying he is concerned it would create dangerous precedents that Democrats would all but certainly use in the future to undermine election integrity...

... "I share the concerns of many Arkansans about irregularities in the presidential election, especially in states that rushed through election-law changes to relax standards for voting-by-mail," Cotton said. "I also share their disappointment with the election

results. I, therefore, support a commission to study the last election and propose reforms to protect the integrity of our elections. And after Republicans win in Georgia, the Senate should also hold more hearings on these matters. All Americans deserve to have confidence in the elections that undergird our free government..."

*... Cotton's statement continues by explaining that he believes **this challenge by Congress to the electoral college is a perversion of the Founders' intent to have the states run elections, not Congress.***

"Nevertheless, the Founders entrusted our elections chiefly to the states -- not Congress. They entrusted the election of our president to the people, acting through the Electoral College -- not Congress," Cotton said. "And they entrusted the adjudication of election disputes to the courts -- not Congress. Under the Constitution and federal law, Congress's power is limited to counting electoral votes submitted by the states."

As such, Cotton said, he believes this could create dangerous precedents that Democrats would all but certainly abuse in the future when it benefitted them politically.

*"If Congress purported to overturn the results of the
Electoral College, it would not only exceed that power
but also establish unwise precedents," Cotton said.*

Are. You. Friggin'. Kidding. Me? We need a commission
to hold hearings and an inquiry into an investigation of a
subcommittee to produce an abstract of a report to verify
the possibility that a strongly worded letter to the NY Times
should be drafted, in triplicate, and circulated to focus groups
for poll testing to make sure that it does not contain language
deemed offensive or inappropriate and then submitted for
crafting into a non-binding resolution. Perfect.

Senator Cotton: What the hell can you be possibly
thinking by invoking the Founders and Framers in discussing "dangerous precedents" when this election was STOLEN
with malice aforethought by a political party, its operatives,
its allies in the media and quite probably aided and abetted
by foreign enemy nations after four years of the very same
people who attempted to sabotage the results of the previous
election?!

You want dangerous precedents? How about locking
down the nation under the pretext of a phony health crisis
in order for Democrat-run states to destroy whatever waffer-
theen firewalls and safeguards were left to make the theft
possible? Or after the in-your-face intimidation and removal
of legal poll watchers, the stopping of the ballot counting and
the trucking in of pallets of counterfeit ballots along with the
rejiggering of electronic votes? Or the GOP state legislators

abrogating their oaths and certifying the fraudulent results? Or the Supreme Court of the United States abrogating its oath by refusing to hear the case?

The nation is coming apart at the seams and you, and clowns like you in Congress and the so-called "conservative" media have this "we'll-get-'em-next-time" attitude in 2022 and 2024 -- as if we'll ever have another honest election again. Then again, they may not ever need to rig the elections after they give amnesty to the 30 million illegal aliens already in country and the millions more ready to jump the Rio Grande as soon as Biden's ventriloquist mouths the words "So help me G-d" at noon on January 20th.

Let's face it; at this stage of the game, this challenge is a Hail Mary. But it has to be done if for no other reason than on moral grounds. More than likely, the greatest crime in our soon-to-be finished history will go unpunished. But it cannot go un-confronted. Let the Enemy and the propagandists say what they want. They're going to anyway. That line about sunshine patriots is particularly applicable here. Whatever happens going forward, let history record who stood with us and who blathered about dangerous precedents.

Tuesday, January 5, 2021

The first moment of truth for the nation has arrived in Georgia. The runoff election for the two senate seats - undoubtedly stolen by the Enemy nine weeks ago along with the presidential election - is today. What more needs to be said? On their side of the ticket, we have a hideous racialist and anti-Semite paired with a sickly-looking low-T puppet of Pooh-Pooh-Xi[88] pulling his strings. On our side of the ledger we have David Perdue and Kelly Loeffler. Yay. No really. I'm ebullient. Go team! -- Mostly to hell, because for decades the GOP has been worse than useless in fighting the gradual nudging, and now sudden shoving of the nation into a socialist mass grave.

Since the ascendancy of Donald Trump, they have proven themselves complicit in the crime. The actions and inaction of Brian Kemp and Brad Raffensperger, as well as their counterparts in the other tainted states, the Supreme Court (except Alito and Thomas), half the GOP House and most of the GOP Senate contingent speak volumes. Chalk it up to the result of decades-long societal and cultural rot, greed or some combination of both, we are in this predicament not so much because of what the Left has done to us, but because the party we have voted for election after election after election has stabbed us in the back each and every time. And here we are, yet again, in Georgia.[89]

What Americans have witnessed over the past four years, as I've written several times, is a textbook example of political power squandered. Republican senators, rather than maximize the unexpected gift of a Republican White House, Senate, and House

---

88 Xi Jinping

89 https://amgreatness.com/2021/01/04/losing-would-be-a-fitting-coda-for-the-feckless-gop-senate/

*of Representatives to advance long-promised "con-
servative" policies, wasted the opportunity while
giving political cover to both the corrupt president
who preceded Donald Trump and the one who will
succeed him...*

*A once-in-a-generation chance to purge the Beltway
of fossilized institutionalists was bypassed. Ditto for
major reforms of immigration law, foreign affairs,
trade agreements, federal regulations, and climate
change activism. The president almost singlehandedly retooled failed national policies through
executive orders or administrative decree; in most
cases, especially related to U.S. military presence
abroad, Senate Republicans thwarted rather than
aided the Trump Administration.*

*"Conservative" achievements over the past four years
belong solely to the president and his team, not to
congressional Republicans.*

*And when Mitt Romney, the junior Republican
senator from Utah and two-time losing Republican presidential candidate, became the first senator
in U.S. history to vote to convict a president of his
own political party, Senate Majority Leader Mitch
McConnell (R-Ky.) did nothing to punish him.
When asked by a reporter if McConnell would expel
Romney from the Republican conference, something*

a Democratic leader would do without a second of hesitation, McConnell only said he was "surprised and disappointed" by Romney's vote...

...And as evidence piled up that officials in several states broke election laws to help Biden win, Senate Republicans were silent. A select group of House Republicans, once again, showed spine by demanding investigations and joining a lawsuit filed by the Texas Attorney General that detailed mail-in ballot fraud in four key states, but invertebrate Senate Republicans, once again, looked the other way. Senator Ron Johnson (R-Wis.) finally held a public hearing into "election irregularities" on December 16 -- better than nothing, but effectively it accomplished nothing.

Now, after undoubtedly getting an earful from their constituents, a dozen Republican senators are attempting a last-minute play to salvage their reputations and mollify the party's infuriated base. Senators Ted Cruz (R-Texas), Josh Hawley (R-Mo.), Marsha Blackburn (R-Tenn.) and others plan to reject certifying the election results on January 6 unless a full audit is conducted...

According to Sasse, Romney, Collins, and others, the real tragedy is not how county election workers manipulated absentee ballots or how unelected bureaucrats in key states blatantly violated state election laws to help Biden win; no, the real tragedy is a president, backed by 75 million American voters, dares to again gum up the corrupt political machinery bent on grinding him (and his supporters) down at any cost.

Trump, in the messy way that is admittedly part of his political brand, is left to fight the powers-that-be alone, recognizing that this battle isn't just about him but about the fate and future of the country as a whole.

As for Cruz and his compatriots, their counterattack is too little, too late. The Senate should have shut down all other business from November 3 on and held one hearing after another on election irregularities and illegalities in the disputed states, demanding action from the Justice Department and state lawmakers. Threats to reject certification should have been made several weeks ago, not a few days before Congress is scheduled to certify the Electoral College vote.

Julie Kelly over at American Greatness napalms the GOP so go read the entire piece. As she alludes, all of this crap tomorrow in Congress might just be the farewell performance of kabuki/bukkake theater. This whole notion of 10 days of hearings just reeks of it. The evidence is clear and has been since election night. Donald Trump was well on his way to at least a 400 electoral vote victory over the Polident-elect until a coordinated attack in several key cities across six states sabotaged and stole the election. We saw it and they saw it. If the situation were reversed, aside from Josh Hawley and his family taken out and beaten to death, do you think the Democrats would have let this go this far? Nine weeks later?

Do not get me wrong; given what is at stake right here and right now, the Senate cannot be allowed to flip over to the Enemy[90]. Putting all our justifiable hatred of the GOP aside, the consequences are almost quite literally life and death. If you are in Georgia, vote - early and often and I'm only half-joking considering the way the Enemy deals with elections.

As Edmund Burke famously quipped, "All that is required for evil to triumph is for good men to do nothing." For sure, he is most definitely not referring to the GOP. He is referring to us. From this day forward. And thanks to the GOP, what we will be required to do to stop this evil is going to be a hell of a lot more difficult than merely pulling the lever in a rigged voting machine.

Wednesday, January 6, 2021

Last night, Ace declared:[91]

Now that polls are closed, [in the Georgia Senate runoff elections] I can say, without actually harming

---

90 Democrat-Media-Deep State Complex

91 http://ace.mu.nu/archives/391995.php#391995

the chances of Republicans winning: I don't care who wins. I am no longer a Republican. I will not care about this shitbag party until it competes for my vote.

And yes, I'm now at the point where I wouldn't mind seeing complete Democrat control for 12 years until the cucks are made to understand that I can defect, too.

While I agree wholeheartedly with the boss's sentiment, in his understandable rage he doesn't see that he, we and whatever recognizable vestige of this nation and our culture that remains is about to be shoved head first into a meat grinder. I can't even imagine the first 12 minutes of Joe-Blow, let alone 12 years of it. As for the GOP competing for our vote, even if we ever have another fair election at any level, which we will not, it is now eminently clear that the GOP could care fuck all for us because it is fully on board with the globalist mission to dismantle and subjugate America, with the Communist Chinese pulling the strings. That is, if more than a billion members of the Religion of Peace have anything to say about that, but that's another story.

Here's something fun to consider:

1. Congress actually does the impossible by rejecting the Biden steal and restoring President Trump.

2. But then, with both chambers in Enemy hands, he is impeached, with no months-long hearings

but on a simple 10-minute up or down floor vote followed in short order by Mike Pence shown the door 10 minutes later.

3. Profit! Malig-Nancy Pelosi is sworn in as the 47th President. Not to worry. Congress won't let us down; they'll certify the election and Biden will be sworn in two weeks from today, so rest easy...

Not to worry. Congress won't let us down; they'll certify the election and Biden will be sworn in two weeks from today, so rest easy... If we're not in it now, we are hurtling towards the abyss. They've captured the government, the courts, the media, and most crucially the schools, where all of this metastasized from so many decades ago. My only consolation is that there are at a minimum over 74 million people who did not vote for this and perhaps twice that number not down with "the struggle" so to speak. Some have stated that the only way to really fight back is to run for office, get involved with school boards and community boards, enter the teaching profession, etc. etc. The problem is, with the Enemy in control of virtually everything, do you think they will now allow voices of dissent within the institutions that took them nearly a century to take over to wrest control away from them?

So, the question remains, how best to organize and focus the potential energy of tens of millions of us into a force to be reckoned with. Actually, the question is, given what I just stated, can it be focused at all into a force to be reckoned with?

The world wonders...

Thursday, January 7, 2021

I cannot even begin to process what happened yesterday in the Capitol. It was without a doubt probably the blackest day at least since 9/11/01 and probably one of the blackest in our now concluded history. If the nation didn't die on Election Day, it certainly was mortally wounded. Yesterday, the executioner delivered the coup de grace. Emphasis on the word "coup."

I have to now choose my words *extremely* carefully for obvious reasons, which are going to be a lot more obvious as the coming days and months pass. I abhor violence. I was brought up by kind, honorable, moral and righteous parents who practiced what they preached in terms of tolerance and compassion. This despite a mother who endured the horrors of actual Nazism, and a father who lost a brother on Saipan courtesy of the Japanese emperor. But the combination of their own upbringing and their life experiences did not preclude them from quite justifiably seeing the world as realists, if not in solid black and white then certainly in distinct and deep shades of darks and lights.

Normally in a situation similar to what we saw yesterday (if one even exists) I would say something like "while I cannot condone what happened, I certainly understand why it happened." For sure, this time I certainly understand it, but thanks to the Left and now the GOP, I am a red nether hair's breadth from crossing the formerly bright red line of the former. In the Bible, from Ecclesiastes "there is a time for peace and a time for war." I have to ask myself, what time is it now?

Shifting gears for a moment, something was awfully strange about the storming of the Capitol Building yesterday by supposed Trump supporters. Oh, no doubt once the barricades were breached, quite a number of actual Trump supporters got inside the House and Senate chambers and offices and caused a ruckus. How could that have even been possible? Well, when D.C. mayor Muriel Bowser told federal law enforcement officers to stand down the day before the protest, you do the math. Ever wonder how Congressional hearings always seem to be invaded by shrieking Code Pinko leftists carrying signs for the benefit of the propagandists' cameras? QED.

Tragically, a victim who has been identified as a Trump supporter was shot and killed in the chaos and confusion. Now the propagandists, the Democrats and the GOP are condemning Trump as well as anyone and everyone who voted for or otherwise support him as traitors, engaging in violent treason and sedition. Given everything we have endured this past year and going back into the Obama years and beyond really, that attitude is risible in the extreme. It's also infuriating beyond my capacity to describe the emotion.

My rage this morning is directed in particular at the GOP. Given everything we have seen and endured, these bastards – with the exception of the handful of patriotic members of the Senate and House who exercised their legitimate Constitutional authority and right to challenge the Electoral College votes – including how Vice President Mike Pence stabbed us in the heart. Correction, they, along with the state legislatures in question as well as the majority on the Supreme Court, stabbed us in the heart weeks if not months ago. Pence, et al. were just twisting the knife. Meh, it happened the moment President Trump said "so help me G-d" four years ago when the GOP controlled both houses of Congress and sabotaged him at every turn for two years, until Paul Ryan delivered the House to Nancy Pelosi.

Year after year, election after election, we begged and pleaded with that party to stop what is now inevitable and imminent from happening. I blame them for what happened yesterday. For what happened nine weeks ago. For what has happened to this country for the past 60 years by not opposing the overthrow of America as founded and going along to get along, either out of denial, greed or some combination of both.

Now there is talk of impeaching Trump, with just under two weeks left, which if successful would ban him for running for president again in 2024, as if any election ever again in this country, such as it is, is ever not going to be rigged by the Enemy. And this vile lout Corey Bush is introducing legislation to have those who moved to challenge the Electoral

College expelled from office. Looking beyond that, do you think that anyone who donated to Trump or to a Republican is not going to have that information leaked to potential employers, or banks or perhaps to the mostly peaceful protesters of Antifa and BLM who will know where you live?

Funny how city after city can burn to the ground as police either willingly or not stand by and let it happen and that was somehow justified. Yet here we are after a year of having our livelihoods as well as our freedoms destroyed on the pretext of a health crisis that was nothing more than a bad flu, and now our only legal and legitimate way to protest this, our sacred right to vote for which thousands of our soldiers, among them my uncle, died to preserve, stolen. And those who had the power and the G-d damn duty to stop it not only abrogated that responsibility but turned around and flamed us for pointing it out and demanding they abide by it.

Regardless of whether it was indeed Trump supporters who started the mayhem or not, I certainly understand how it happened, and G-d help me for saying it, I'm just about to the point of condoning it. It is obvious for anyone with eyes to see and a mind to process it that we no longer have a legitimate government, nor do we have legitimate political institutions or regular order. For anyone on our side to blame Trump or us for what happened is the last straw, along with the certification of Joe-Blow as the legitimate winner of the 2020 election.

I cannot believe what we have witnessed yesterday and really since the national incarceration/lockdowns. I am grateful that I do not have children, mostly because I would have dreaded them having to try and exist in a tyranny or worse, having been brainwashed in the schools into cheering it on.

I'm too enraged to weep. They have sown the wind and they are going to reap a whirlwind.

Friday, January 8, 2021

The fallout over Black Wednesday continues. That was the day that America was snuffed out for good by Enemies domestic and foreign (I'm looking right at the monstrous Chi-Coms). Naturally, like slavery, Jim Crow, real insurrection, poverty, domestic terrorism and every other misery they have inflicted for 244 years, they cast the blame on us for what happened on that day while strutting, preening and usurping the mantle of righteously aggrieved. And you can bet every last red cent of your $600 federal stimulus insult they will continue to grind that designer jackboot in our collective face until the end of time.

My heart aches for those who lost their life or were injured that day including Ashli Babbit, a 14-year military veteran who came to Washington like thousands of other decent, patriotic Americans to show their outrage at a stolen election to an uncaring and indifferent Congress. A Congress that when the dust had settled put a seal of approval on the greatest crime in the history of the country formerly known as the United States of America. However, the chaos of storming the Capitol building happened, and there is growing evidence to indicate that Antifa/BLM thug terrorists were let into the building with the actual assistance of Capitol Police officers, and I applaud it.

When these same BLM/Antifa thug terrorists beat people up, riot, loot, vandalize monuments, burn buildings and decimate entire communities on the completely false pretext of "systemic racism" they are lauded as heroes by the Democrat-Enemy and their propagandists. Their violence and destruction are either deemed justified in the context of that false narrative or labeled peaceful or patriotic when the flames and bricks accidentally make it onto your TV screen. And that's just what's been happening since last May when some criminal named Floyd died while being arrested.

The armed militant wings of the Democrat Party have been burning, looting, occupying and terrorizing our cities and towns, including allegedly sacrosanct government buildings for years with not even a peep of protest from the usual suspects. Funny how no one mentions the antics of Code Pinko (who are given guest passes by Democrat politicians) every time there is a Congressional hearing, let alone *the 1954 attack by Puerto Rican terrorists who shot up the House of Representatives.*[92]

Didn't that shambling, cackling gin blossom Hillary Clinton declare dissent to be patriotic? I guess it is unless you're dissenting anything that aids and abets the Left. When you think about it, the presidency of Donald Trump

---

92 https://www.c-span.org/video/?317988-2/1954-shooting-congress

was a giant dissent against the intentional sabotage, dismantling and selling out of this nation that had gone essentially unimpeded since at least the end of World War Two. Beyond the petty and personal, the real reason they hate President Trump – forever my beloved and revered President Trump – is because they fear him. He was an existential threat to their graft, corruption and lust for absolute power because he was an incorruptible outsider that remained that way. So he had to be destroyed. And in his (seeming) destruction by way of impeachment and finally the theft of his clear victory, a Luca Brasi dead-fish-in-a-flak-vest message was sent to anyone who might want to follow in his footsteps. The question is, will we get that message? Will Trump, by way of the undeniable movement if not consciousness-lifting of millions of us, remain an existential threat to the forces that have now enslaved us?

Rush Limbaugh returned to the airwaves yesterday (thank G-d) and despite his illness blasted out much of what I have been saying regarding the complete hypocrisy of the Enemy and their apologists regarding the so-called "riots." It was comforting to hear him again, especially after Black Wednesday, but about my only point of contention was his explanation of why so many GOPers and Trump cabinet members and staff are now jumping ship and abandoning the President. Per Rush, it is to preserve their future status in D.C. While I do not disagree insofar as in any other time than this, once you've done your time in an administration, there's always a job waiting at a think tank, media outlet, lobbying firm or university where you can park your ass by day and then hit the cocktail party circuit by night. Not this time. Anyone who served with Trump in any capacity at best will be persona non grata, even if they go on TV day after day doing POW hostage videos denouncing him. At worst, they might get the Paul Manafort treatment, or even the Steve Scalise treatment depending on the circumstances and their particular "crime against the state" between 2017 and 2021. Even before the (s)election, rabid lickspittle cockroaches like Robert Reich were demanding re-education camps for Trump supporters and now we have calls for those who initiated the Electoral College protest to be expelled from Congress. Do I even have to go into the mass censorship campaign of dissenting voices, including the President himself?

In any case, and I guess it comes down to one's own personality and degree of intestinal fortitude and morality, but that so few of his allies are refusing to stand with him and speak the truth about the events of Black Wednesday is understandable, yet no less tragic in the extreme. I guess I shouldn't really pass judgment unless my house has been firebombed by mostly peaceful storm-troopers. Still, it's bad enough that a national election as well as now two senate seats in Georgia were stolen in front of our eyes. Provably with reams of hard and anecdotal evidence. But those who stole it are not just your ordinary, garden variety FDR or Harry Truman Democrats but corrupt power-mad agents of Communist China or brainwashed, racialist Maoists out to enslave us and eradicate the last vestiges of our culture.

Bad enough to have to endure the noxious emissions from the festering cakeholes of such vermin as Chuck Schumer and Nancy Pelosi, but to hear Republicans going on and on about the violation of sacred Democratic institutions, and the sanctity of the hallowed halls of Congress and the defiling of our Constitutional heritage is just the bitter end. Where the hell were you when cities burned? Where were you when we were locked down and prevented from seeking comfort in our churches and synagogues? Where were you when our children were kept locked out of schools (bad as they are)? Where were you when the backbone of our prosperity, small businesses, were crushed and destroyed? Where the hell were you for two whole years when this President tried to dismantle Obamacare, secure our borders, bring our troops home from useless Middle Eastern meat grinders, and institute policies that would finally get the ball rolling on devolving power away from D.C. and back to the people? And where the hell were you when the toilet paper-thin safeguards against election fraud were stripped away in the statehouses and the courts and then finally, when the chips were down, when it really mattered, to put an end to this madness and do your duty by reversing the steal?

You have the fucking unmitigated temerity to blood libel this president and the tens of millions of us who voted for him by hiding behind a supposedly besmirched Constitution and defiled Capitol building? No. By your inaction in the face of naked tyranny, and actions to legitimize the bastardization of the rule of law, it is all of you that are guilty of the crimes you unconvincingly shriek "j'accuse!" at Trump and all of us.

I don't know which BLM/Antifa goon or apologist said, referring to the horrendous Dresden-like destruction of property in Kenosha or Portland or Minneapolis, "hey, it's only a building." Considering what the Democrats and their confederates in the GOP have done while inside the Capitol for years now, "hey, it's only a building."

Tuesday, January 12, 2021

The nightmare grows deeper and darker. Yesterday, Ace highlighted the completely unsurprising announcement from humanoid doughboy Ed Morrissey that he is now officially a Democrat because of what happened on Black Wednesday. It seems to be indicative of a trend with conservative media types insofar as a shift in tone from a state of denial with laughably ridiculous "we'll get 'em next time in '22 and '24" pablum, to frothing at the mouth damnations of Trump and the tens of millions of us who support him. Forget the nearly four-year run of the most positively transformative presidency in American history as well as an electoral victory that was hijacked in front of our eyes. Because he and we dared to stage a protest on Capitol Hill- mostly aimed at a Republican Party that was acting as a conspirator to the steal after the fact – that also was hijacked by the Left and turned into a Reichstag Fire incident, he and we are to be scapegoated and blood-libeled for all time.

Even that is tame in comparison to what it sets the stage for. It's bad enough that clueless, effete Ivy League "elites" — retreads from previous administrations and their nepot spawn whose brainstems have been pickled in Howard Zinn and the 1619 Project – are about to kick-start the Leviathan from its four years in mothballs and destroy what's left of our already lockdown-strangled economy while once again bowing down to the world's tyrants and terrorists. That's just business as usual when Democrats quote-unquote "win" elections from Republicans.

Because we dared stand athwart history and not only yell "stop!" but for a few shining years manage to put the machine in reverse, we have unleashed what David Horowitz at Frontpage Mag so aptly describes as "the totalitarian screaming to get out" from inside every progressive. Every instrumentality of a thoroughly corrupt government as well as its fascistic cronies in the pseudo-private sector are about to be brought to bear on anyone who challenges their authority or their official story.[93]

You had better believe there are discussions among credit card companies, banks, and other financial institutions about punishing organizations they view as opposing leftist political views. In December, for example, a so-far unnamed credit card processing company refused to process donations to the American Family Association because it is socially conservative.

93 https://thefederalist.com/2021/01/11/big-corporate-uses-capitol-riots-to-push-communist-style-social-credit-system-on-americans/

Previously, big banks refused to bank for legal gun manufacturers after pressure from leftist activists.

This is the kind of power the left holds over all the institutions that make life possible for Americans, and they have already revealed they are not afraid to flex that power against the left's chosen enemies. All of this is merely the next step in years of campaigns to use economic pressure to control public policy...

...We all saw Big Tech and Big Media collude to hide information damaging to the left and amplify information and narratives damaging to the right. Corporations are now wielding supra-governmental power untethered by even the pretense of constitutional legitimacy, and our government seems entirely powerless to stop them.

This all moves us closer to a nongovernmental social credit system like that employed by Communist China, which economically and socially punishes people for "wrongthink." It appears that global oligarchs have decided to not only collude with China's totalitarian control over its society, but to export that social control to formerly free nations such as the United States...

...This week's escalation of totalitarian speech controls and witch hunts — Are you now or have

you ever been a supporter of Donald Trump? — is terrifying, and not just because of the lack of defenses against leftists 'demonstrated control of information and funding. If they can do this to the president of the United States, who can't these corporations do it to?

If President Trump had actually called for rioters to stop and "go home in peace," and firmly denounced violent lawbreaking while acknowledging the 99.9999999% of his supporters who are peaceful and lawful, but these corporations told the world he was instead "inciting violence" and encouraging "sedition," how would we ever know the truth?

If they choose to lie to us, to lie about one political party, to lie about events they use to impose draconian speech and social controls, and to ban us from ever sharing information that proves or even simply suggests they lied or aren't telling the whole story, how would we ever know it?

From Jack Cashill at American Thinker:[94]

Reportedly, Louisiana Governor Huey Long was once asked, "Do you think we will ever have Fascism in America?" Said Long, "Sure, only we'll call it

---

94 https://www.americanthinker.com/articles/2021/01/president_trump_takes_a_hit_for_the_team.html

anti-Fascism." *What Trump exposed, and which may prove of more lasting value than what he accomplished, was the real-life unfolding of Long's paradox...*

... The "fascist" movement began with Italy's Benito Mussolini. He took the name of his party from the Latin word fasces meaning a bundle of rods gathered together in one strong hand. Starting in ten days all the rods will be gathered — the presidency, the House, the Senate, Big Tech, Big Media, Hollywood, the CIA, the FBI, perhaps even the military. Just in the last few weeks, their collective eagerness to suppress dissent has shown up their mentors in the CCP.

To enforce the new order at the street level, the Left has developed its own private army. In a marvelous bit of self-parody, the bully boys of the new fascism, the Left's own SA, call themselves anti-fascists or Antifa for short. Huey Long had the last laugh on that one.

With his back to the wall, Trump rallied the last bulwark against this encroaching tyranny, the American people. In so doing, he showed the comically obvious hypocrisy of the Left's support for "largely peaceful" protests.

Although events this past week did not appear to work out as we might have liked, appearances can be deceiving. There were lessons learned, eyes opened. It seems somehow providential that the people's protest at the "People's House" occurred on the Epiphany.

Only a few short months ago, we sort of half-jokingly discussed "grabbing the upper bunk in gulag fun camp." It's not a joke any more. The Left has engaged in physical violence from assault and murder of individuals to mass rioting and civil unrest that have lain waste to at least a dozen urban areas. They have suspended Constitutional rights on the pretext of a health crisis that is provably only slightly more deadly than seasonal flu. They have rigged and/or stolen elections with the complicity of lawmakers and jurists that looked the other way and blamed the whistleblowers. To merely dissent, protest or utter an opinion deemed not in keeping with Leftist dogma is to be a terrorist, seditionist, and all the way down to subhuman who should be exterminated. Sound familiar?

I'm always an optimist but things are going to get very dark and very quickly. G-d help us.

Wednesday, January 13, 2021

If you thought the de-platforming, censorship and demonization in the wake of the Black Wednesday false flag "riot" was frightening enough, you ain't seen nothing yet.

With one week until marionette meat puppet Zhou Bai-Din [Joe Biden] is installed as president of the country formerly known as the United States of America, things are happening that are scaring what's left of the living shit out of me. Let's make this perfectly clear for the trolls and other sub-imbeciles to understand: the invasion of the Capitol Building was a pre-planned operation coordinated by the Democrats and their armed militant terrorist death squad Antifa with the cooperation of the Capitol Police in order to create an incident that smeared President Trump and the many thousands of peaceful orderly citizens protesting the theft of the 2020 election. A few dozen who foolishly followed the confederate wolves in MAGA clothing were not exactly doing the typical Democrat "mostly peaceful rioting" while, tragically, Ashli Babbitt was murdered in cold blood by a Capitol cop (say her name, right?).

The tragic loss of life of Babbitt and three others notwithstanding, what happened was the equivalent of what one pundit described as nothing more than a "panty raid." Forgetting the *B*urning, *L*ooting and *M*urdering that decimated at least a dozen cities since last May, forgetting the fact that Democrats, their media propagandists and cheerleaders in the entertainment industry, the brainwashing mills of academia and vast swathes of corporate America justified all of it based on the most titanic lie since the Jewish blood libel – America as an illegitimate, irredeemably evil white supremacist nation – what happened one week ago now justifies not only the immediate removal of President Trump from office but the removal from the public square of anyone and everyone who was either in D.C. at the rally, voiced approval of that rally or voices an opinion supporting the undeniable truth that is the basis for that rally: the theft of the 2020 election.

The thousands of peaceful people in D.C. that day as well as the tens of millions of people who know it, and are justifiably angry. They're angry not only because it was stolen but because our cries for justice and redress of grievance to those who had the ability and the duty to mete that justice out not only refuse to hear them, but have now openly turned on us. More on that in a moment.

Now, despite confirmation that the half-naked chucklehead dressed up like a headhunting shaman from New Guinea was a leftist environmental whacko[95] and another alleged MAGA minion was actually a BLM terrorist who had a trail of violent eliminationist rhetoric against Trump and his supporters,[96] the FBI – yay!!! – is about to "round up the usual suspects" because of two live (allegedly) pipe bombs that were found in D.C. during Black Wednesday. And when I say the usual suspects, of course I'm not referring to the aforementioned hard leftists; I mean ordinary citizens who were merely in attendance at the rally. Scape, meet goat.[97]

Federal law enforcement officials also revealed that pipe bombs found on the U.S. Capitol grounds last

95 https://thenationalpulse.com/exclusive/capitol-antagonist-climate-change/

96 https://thefederalist.com/2021/01/17/federal-judge-releases-blm-capitol-rioter-without-bail/

97 https://www.dailywire.com/news/fbi-capitol-pipe-bombs-had-explosive-igniters-hundreds-of-arrests-expected-in-capitol-attack

Wednesday, were equipped with explosive igniters, they do not know why the bombs did not explode, and that finding the bomber, who appears in some surveillance footage taken outside the Capitol, is a top priority for the FBI.

Acting US Attorney for D.C. Michael Sherwin said Tuesday that the FBI has already opened 160 separate cases as a result of last week's riot and assault and that the FBI expects "hundreds; of criminal cases to be filed against people who participated in the Capitol riot within the next several weeks," according to Fox News.

The agency plans to make the probe a "long-term investigation," and one FBI official, Washington Field Office ADIC Steven D'Antuono told reporters that he wanted "to stress that the FBI has a long memory and a broad reach."

Sherwin added that his office is planning to be involved with the FBI "for the long haul." "This is going to be a long-term investigation," *he said.*

Emphasis mine in that last quote. I could have sworn I saw a link about Sherwin being fully on board with the Russia collusion hoax/smear against President Trump but surprise-surprise it seems to have been airbrushed off of the internet. No matter. The FBI is a corrupt organization that works at the behest of the Democrat-Globalist-ChiCom Enemy. Along with the equally corrupt DOJ of which it is a part, it has been involved in all sorts of schemes to railroad innocent people for decades. It serves no purpose other than to advance itself and its political allies/enablers with total disregard for ethics, the rule of law and the Constitution. If they can ruin people like Michael Flynn, Paul Manafort, Ted Stevens and the two saps who spent decades in prison so that Whitey Bulger can galavant around with Bob Mueller, surely they can plant a couple of prop pipe bombs as a pretext to round up a few dozen citizens and make them confess, pour encourager les autres.

Thursday, January 14, 2021

The complete and utter sham of a second impeachment of perhaps one of the greatest presidents in history – and quite possibly the last – tops the news. I'd say our government is a joke but for the fact that yesterday's Roman farce merely confirms that it's dead. The pretext for the Enemy to seize absolute power underscores one of the greatest political aphorisms of our time, from the mind of none other than Ace[98] himself:

Our speech is violence, their violence is speech.

And of course, when there is no violence, the Enemy will plop on a MAGA hat, wrap themselves in a Gadsden

---

98 www.ace.mu.nu

flag, initiate some, then blame it on us, as was the case on Black Wednesday. For me to get all worked up about corrupt degenerates on the left and pseudo-right in D.C., in the propaganda organs or in show biz and everywhere in between strutting, preening and foaming at the mouth with their sub-literate drivel is a waste of time. What I am worked up about is that rigging an election and overthrowing the country merely to seize power is not the end game. It's just the opening gambit. Forget about what's in store in terms of laws and edicts handed down from the rogue's gallery of hardcore Marxist freaks, geeks and thugs that now control the Legislative and Executive branches with little to fear from an, at best, neutered Judiciary.

Any opposition will now be considered seditious and subject to imprisonment. Think that that's hyperbole? Think again:[99]

> *During a live stream on her Instagram page, Ocasio-Cortez was asked by a viewer if, to help with national healing, there were congressional plans to institute any "truth and reconciliation or media literacy initiatives."*
>
> *The socialist congresswoman replied that, yes, indeed, she and some of her colleagues have been exploring media literacy initiatives to help "rein in" the press and combat misinformation after last week's riot at the U.S. Capitol.*

---

99 www.ace.mu.nu

"It's one thing to have differentiating opinions but it's another thing entirely to just say things that are false," Ocasio-Cortez added. "So that's something that we're looking into."

Oh, are they?

Now, perhaps in the political systems favored by AOC citizens are impelled to look to government for ultimate truth, but that's not the case in the United States. At least, not yet. Here, the Constitution "reins in" Congress from intruding on the speech of citizens, journalists, or any private institutions, not the other way around.

We need only point to our media "factcheckers," journalists with political and ideological biases who have regularly, and arbitrarily, labeled completely debatable contentions as falsehoods, while either ignoring or justifying scores of other unsettled contentions. Are these the arbiters of facts who will be manning the government commission appointed by those storied truth-tellers in congress?...

... For those unaware, the "truth and reconciliation commission" the AOC fan asked about was most famously used in South Africa after the fall of apartheid as means of "restorative justice." The insinuation by those who use this phrase is that 74 million

Americans who voted for the Republican presiden-
tial candidate are racist thugs in need for similar
programs. It's a disgusting smear, and speaks to the
dangerous and illiberal inclination of progressives.

Not so long ago, 2008 to be precise, a number of people were raising the alarm bells about the then Democrat candidate for the president and his connections to some of the most rabidly anti-American radicals including Bill Ayers, the former head of the Weathermen terrorists, whose bombs left a trail of bodies and terror from coast to coast in an attempt to overthrow the government. Larry Grathwohl, a Vietnam vet managed to infiltrate the group and became an FBI informer. He recalled sitting in on one of their meetings in the early 70s in what the author of this piece (a tribute to Grathwohl after his death in 2013) described as "a kind of Wannsee Conference at which WUO [Weather Underground Organization] members plotted the murder of 25 million Americans."[100]

I brought up the subject of what's going to happen
after we take over the government: we become
responsible then for administrating 250 million
people. And there was no answers. No one had given
any thought to economics, how you're going to clothe
and feed these people.

---

[100] https://archives.frontpagemag.com/fpm/larry-grathwohl-requiem-american-hero-matthew-vadum/

The only thing that I could get was that they expected that the Cubans and the North Vietnamese and the Chinese and the Russians would all want to occupy different portions of the United States.

They also believed that their immediate responsibility would be to protect against what they called the counter revolution and they felt that this counter revolution could best be guarded against by creating and establishing reeducation centers in the Southwest where they would take all the people who needed to be reeducated into the new way of thinking and teach them how things were going to be.

I asked, well, what is going to happen to those people that we can't reeducate that are diehard capitalists and the reply was that they'd have to be eliminated. And when I pursued this further they estimated that they would have to eliminate 25 million people in these reeducation centers. And when I say eliminate I mean kill — 25 million people.

I want you to imagine sitting in a room with 25 people most of which have graduate degrees from Columbia and other well-known educational centers and hear them figuring out the logistics for the elimination of 25 million people and they were dead serious."

One chilling idea WUO leaders entertained was working enemies of the revolution to death in labor camps, something many so-called progressives today would no doubt favor doing to Tea Party supporters.

And here we are in 2021. The heirs of Ayers, BLM and Antifa, have bombed, napalmed and lain waste to at least a dozen cities across the nation, only this time with the approval of, and quite probably at the behest of the Democrat Party, with the same goal: the overthrow and destruction of the United States. And once again, Ivy League eggheads with doctorates are talking about re-education camps. And Bill Ayers[101] is still tied at the hip to Barack Hussein Obama. And Barack Hussein Obama orchestrated the coup that wound up not only sabotaging President Trump, but finally overthrowing a nation, society and a people that he despises.

When Alexandria Ocasio-Cortez blathers on about "truth and reconciliation" commissions, and Robert Reich as well as other incompetent little Eichmanns of his ilk parroting Ayers and foaming at the mouth in orgasmic anticipation of "re-education camps," to laugh at this – especially in light of what we have seen with our own eyes this past year – is to be dangerously out of touch. As sick and twisted as these people are, they have captured the government and all its instrumentalities of law enforcement. There are no more firewalls. The only thing that can sate a will to power is absolute power.

Dangerous times ahead.

---

101 https://www.discoverthenetworks.org/individuals/bill-ayers

Friday, January 15, 2021

While the top story may be the news that broke last night announcing President Trump's declassifying of Obamagate documents concerning the Hillary Clinton bought-and-paid-for Steele Dossier, the most significant story I think is the Enemy's vote to impeach the President with just scant days remaining in his term. Aside from mere foaming at the mouth rabid hatred of this man, arguably one of the greatest natural leaders and patriots the nation formerly known as America ever produced, there is a rationale behind it: to break the back of the American revival/anti-globalist groundswell that carried him to victory in 2016 **AND 2020.**

Beyond its uselessness in practical terms of removing the President prior to noon this coming Wednesday, I think it is a colossal political blunder. If stealing the national election and quite possibly both chambers of Congress wasn't enough, blood-libeling the President and by extension all of us as violent, racist insurrectionists for a "riot" in the Capitol that was caused by agents of the Democrats, and then impeaching him is an absolute outrage. And for key figures in the GOP and far too many backbenchers to willingly go along with this just underscores the futility of conventional party politics, if not explodes it as the myth that it is.

But the premeditated murder of the greatest nation on earth cannot go unanswered. It must not go unanswered. Somehow, some way, some day, there must be some righteous retribution where this nation is restored, the wicked are

THE END OF AMERICA

punished, the corrupt system they ran dismantled and destroyed, and safeguards introduced that prevent this cancer from ever infecting us again. Call it "fundamental transformation," if you will. Sadly, I do not think I will live long enough to see it happen, but we have no choice but to fight.

Until that time, we and our children will face a domestic feral Leviathan that will use its power to control and coerce every aspect of our lives in order to maintain absolute power while lining the pockets of those in charge, as well as a cultural and academic system that played perhaps the central role in putting us in this position. As bad as that is, there's also the totalitarian regime in the Orient hell-bent on global hegemony via bribery, espionage and perhaps overt military action, which we will be powerless to stop even if we wanted, considering an alarming number of our political leaders have been in their pocket for years.

I'm not going to lie to you; the situation is very much in doubt.[102]

> *Oswald Spengler's The Decline of The West, published 1918-1922, laid out the trajectory of the enfeeblement and decay that awaited us, developing a theme that went as far back as the Greek historian Polybius, but that, in the wake of a war that wiped out a generation, seemed less a "theme" than an historically imminent reality. The greatest poet of the modern age, William Butler Yeats, felt it in his bones, working*

102 https://www.americanthinker.com/articles/2021/01/are_the_end_times_near_.html

out a visionary schematism in his prose volume A Vision and reflecting on the inevitable in his timeless poem "The Second Coming," written one year after the end of the Great War: "And what rough beast, its hour come round at last/Slouches toward Bethlehem to be born?" Robert Bork's must-read Slouching Towards Gomorrah hammers out Yeats's vision in lurid contemporary detail, pointing toward a "syndrome" of collectivist attitudes dominating the culture, the debilitation of the family structure, and a "left-liberal moral consensus" diluting the text of the U.S. Constitution...

...In the course of time, cowards and parasites — let us call it the Iscariot function — will prevail over Great Men and Women. Nation-saviors like Churchill and Thatcher will be cast aside, heroes like Trump will be betrayed by friends and colleagues and openly cheated of re-election. The historical template is Themistocles, the philosophical, Socrates, and the literary, Shakespeare's. They cannot forestall the vector of decline and will be derided and punished for having tried to do so. As Adams wrote in an April 22, 1776 letter to James Warren, "But I fear, that in every assembly, Members will obtain an Influence, by Noise not sense. By Meanness, not Greatness. By Ignorance not Learning. By contracted Hearts not large souls. I fear too, that it will be impossible to

convince and persuade People to establish wise Regulations." And thus do nations and ultimately the civilizations of which they form part subside and vanish as a result of inward rot, the great baulks of timber that hold them up gnawed and crumbling in a myriad of different places.

History, so to speak, can happen here. It has been happening for some considerable time, culminating in the most recent of a long sequence of hammer blows: the fraudulent election of Joe Biden thanks to widespread electoral malfeasance, the advent of rigorous and pervasive censorship protocols, and the ongoing purge of constitutional freedoms. Indeed, it is happening throughout the Western world. Nonetheless, for those of us who still care and recognize the precious muniment we have been given, let the coup de grace happen later instead of sooner. The fight continues on myriad fronts.

Not exactly "happy and peppy and bursting with love" today, am I? And yet, nothing is inevitable. There is still at a minimum a clear (if not vast) majority of people in this country who are not "down for the struggle." 80 million of them, or more, voted to stop the insanity by supporting Trump and the MAGA/America first agenda. This is no longer about party politics. Party politics is dead. This is about good versus evil.

I'm here, and I'm not going anywhere. Come and get me.

Tuesday, January 19, 2021

I remember a comedian (Byron Allen?), back when we had actual comedians and not clown-nosed cultural revolutionaries, who said: "I'm not afraid of flying. I'm afraid of plummeting on fire from 30,000 feet to a horrible death." Difficult as it is to describe my emotional state, I think that that comes close. As of noon tomorrow, it's going to be pedal to the metal on every horrendous, crackpot leftist/Socialist policy agenda imaginable, both foreign and domestic that has ever been tried before and proven to be at best a fiasco and at worst a lingering disaster — inflicted a thousand-fold on a horrified, unwilling and extremely angry majority of people. That's the plummeting on fire from 30,000 feet part.

The horrible death part is uncharted territory, at least in this country, or what was this country since the United States of America as founded ceased to exist as of Black Wednesday. I'm referring to the purging from the public square of all voices of opposition and dissent to what is now the official regime line. That is, anything that goes against or protests any Democrat, Leftist, Progressive, Socialist dogma, meme or policy, from the legitimacy of "Polident-elect Zhou Bai-Din"[103] to the insanity of men in dresses having access to female restrooms to the joys of post-natal infanticide to melanin as Caucasian kryptonite and everything in between.

---

103 Joe Biden

It's funny, as in disgustingly hypocritical, how the Left always yammers on about multiple perspectives, how truth is purely subjective and how we cannot judge other cultures or societies through the lens of our own. Yes, tolerance, acceptance and that nauseating "Co-Exist" bumper sticker are their watchwords. And yet when it comes to anyone or anything that challenges them, they are so thoroughly intolerant, inflexible and absolutist in their belief that they are right than the most radical fundamentalist Tora-Bora cave-dweller enrolled at Embry Riddle (you can almost sense a theme here).

When odious, dim louts like Steve Cohen put forth a meme that National Guardsmen are not to be trusted because the vast majority is white, male and did not vote – to the best of their knowledge (nudge-nudge wink-wink) – for Biden, it goes beyond the mere smearing of their politics, gender and race. He is not very subtly condemning them, and by extension all of us, as criminal enemies of "our democracy" (puke), meaning the regime. And that condemnation is a green light to all the thugs of BLM, Antifa and the James Hodgkinsons[104] out there to take action.

Worse than that, it lays the groundwork for enabling acts of the sort last seen in the wake of the 1933 Reichstag Fire. Outlawing of opposition political parties, silencing of opposition media outlets and potentially mass arrests and show trials of opposition political leaders (not that the GOP-e is an opposition party in any sense of the word) and ultimately

104 https://www.foxnews.com/politics/scalise-shooter-appeared-to-be-bernie-sanders-campaign-volunteer

private citizens who dare speak out. Anyone who thinks that that's crazy talk is not paying attention.

"Brace for impact."

Wednesday, January 20, 2021

The stations of uncensored expression are closing down; the lights are going out; but there is still time for those to whom freedom... mean[s] something, to consult together. Let me, then, speak in truth and earnestness while time remains... ...A state of society where men may not speak their minds, where children denounce their parents to the police, where a business man or small shopkeeper ruins his competitor by telling tales about his private opinions; such a state of society cannot long endure if brought into contact with the healthy outside world. The light of civilised progress with its tolerances and co-operation, with its dignities and joys, has often in the past been blotted out. But I hold the belief that we have now at last got far enough ahead of barbarism to control it, and to avert it, if only we realise what is afoot and make up our minds in time. We shall do it in the end. But how much harder our toil for every day's delay!

—Winston Churchill, October 16, 1938,
Broadcast to the United States from London[105]

---

105 https://www.nationalchurchillmuseum.org/the-lights-are-going-out.html

In a few short hours, we are going to enter a phase of our lives where we will be confronted with situations, perhaps even of life and death, that are going to challenge us in ways that until recently seemed unimaginable. Not just physically and emotionally but in ways that will force us to confront who we are and what we believe as rational, decent, G-d fearing human beings. If anyone thinks this is hyperbole, you have not been paying attention to what has been happening all around us for the past four years and longer. Check that; it's more likely that those who had not been paying attention at all would be stunned at the implications of things like re-education camps and de-programming of conservatives, purging of our armed forces of anyone with impure thoughts (i.e. pro-American), businesses firing employees or refusing to serve customers for mere political affiliations, a daughter mocking her mother for being beaten up in D.C. on Black Wednesday and getting her fired because she protested the election theft, and on and on and on.[106]

Just to be clear, it is not Orwell's 1984, it is the Soviet Union of 1937 returned from the hereafter with a human face. There will be no Gulags; millions of people will not be executed. The dissidents will be dealt with "humanely." They will be purged from the universities, media, government jobs, and major corporations. The Bolsheviks; motto, "who does not

106 https://www.americanthinker.com/articles/2021/01/america_a_country_of_victorious_socialism_.html

work does not eat," will be replaced with a new one — "who does not obey does not eat."

Dissent will be suppressed by a brute force of government agencies, including the power of the DOJ to bring frivolous lawsuits and bankrupt its victims and destroy their families...

... The ubiquitous sentinel of American democracy infamous for its colossal failures, the FBI, will regularly discover plots against the government, find caches of weapons and fabricate preposterous accusations against political opponents. As a deterrent, they will be given harsh sentences. The administration will harness every incident to seize greater control over the nation.

The people and businesses are beginning to fear the all-powerful government that is perfectly willing to deploy a full arsenal of state weaponry, such as DOJ, FBI, IRS, EPA, DOE and its powerful FERC (Federal Energy Regulatory Commission), DHS (Department of Homeland Security), DOL (Department of Labor), and other assets we may not know about. The corporations got the message, ending contributions to the Republican Party...

... The Bolsheviks' aphorism: "We can only have two parties: one in power, the other in prison" will be

replaced with "one in power, the other a permanent second-tier loser" assigned to maintain an image of the two-party system.

Neither education nor life experience has prepared Americans for grasping the epochal shift that took place this November. It is not surprising. From ancient times, the most tragic events of history have been triggered by people who, despite the obvious, failed to forecast the future.

And now, we have the National Guard – impugned and maligned by the Dems as perhaps infiltrated by "white supremacists" of questionable loyalty – guarding a sham inauguration behind barbed wire fences. It's a phony media stunt, but one that as Daniel Greenfield states has a more malevolent purpose.[107]

D.C. isn't under military guard to protect our government, but a partisan political agenda.

The Democrats didn't want troops in D.C. when their own were rioting during President Trump's inauguration or violently attacking the White House. They don't need 25,000 troops to stop a few hundred protesters. They need them as a show of force to suppress political opposition.

---

107 https://www.frontpagemag.com/fpm/2021/01/fascist-democrats-are-using-manu-factured-emergency-daniel-greenfield/

Biden and the Democrats are using a military deploy-ment for a show of political force, using a manu-factured crisis to rally support behind their radical agenda, while suppressing dissent...

...America is not a banana republic. There is no place for military theater, lists of enemies, or declaring political opponents to be enemies of the state. The Democrats have already embraced fascism before even formally taking power. Fascists always claim to be seizing power in reaction to an emergency. The manufactured emergency is here. The power grab comes next.

I dread the future, but I am eternally grateful for President Donald Trump. Now more than ever, as the Enemy and Judases like Mitch McConnell try to eradicate him even after he leaves the White House, seemingly for the last time, they will not destroy what he started. A popular movement to restore this nation as founded as the beacon of freedom and the last best hope for a civilized, peaceful world.

Sir Edward Grey, the British Foreign Secretary, on the eve of the First World War, lamented to his friend, "the lamps are going out all over Europe. We shall not see them lit again in our lifetime."

The lamps are going out all over America. G-d be with us.

Thursday, January 21, 2021

I'm numb. I really don't know that I have the koy'ech[108] to do this today, and when I realize I've got another 1,460 days after today I want to go stick my head in an oven. Then again, considering the dreck I'm wading through from yesterday, I'm sure there are quite a few Biden boosters eager to lay their "heeling" hands on my neck and give me a Cass Sunstein patented nudge.

What those who actually decided to torture themselves saw in D.C. yesterday was Dave "Iowahawk" Burge's[109] saying writ large:

1. *Identify a respected institution.*

2. *Kill it.*

3. *Gut it.*

4. *Wear its carcass as a skin suit, while demanding respect.*

If that doesn't encapsulate what the Democrat/Enemy has done to this country since time immemorial, and most assuredly yesterday, I don't know what does.

---

108 Strength, in Yiddish.

109 Alas, Burge devolved into a raving NeverTrumper, but this gem nevertheless remains a 100-megaton truth nuke.

Katie Hopkins witnessed yesterday firsthand:[110]

> *It feels numb here, like watching surgery on your own hand when you are anesthetized against the pain, but can still see the knife cutting flesh and watch your own blood flow. That's exactly what it is like in D.C. Without people, there is no emotion. And without emotion, no one can feel anything. And just like surgery, it feels unreal.*

> *It is emotion that makes these events matter. And there is none to be had here. This is a sterilized inauguration in a city sanitized by a garrison of troops. All you can feel is numb.*

> *Biden stepped up to the podium, on an empty stand, addressing a mall void of life and spoke of his hopes for unity:*

>> "This is our moment of crises and challenge. And unity is the only path forward... Let's start afresh. Let's start to listen to one another, see one another, hear one another."

> *I look around at all the facemasks and muted mouths. And feel my eyes roll in their sockets.*

---

110 https://www.frontpagemag.com/fpm/2021/01/i-watched-bidens-inauguration-first-hand-katie-hopkins/

"We must reject a culture in which facts are manipulated and manufactured."

I remember those suitcases of ballots being hauled out from under tables in Pennsylvania, and the statistically improbably vote dumps in the swing states, and wonder how this old man is not choking on his words.

"America has to be better than this. Just look around. Here we stand in the shadow of the Capitol dome. We endured. We prevailed."

I look around just as he asks us to do, and I see how barren it all is. This man is all but alone with his lies. Nothing has prevailed here, not joy, not emotion, and certainly not the will of the American people.

Daniel Greenfield also nails it:[111]

There were no crowds, just soldiers. After the military and police contingent, the second largest group there for the inauguration weren't Biden's civilian supporters, but his propagandists. With few people, the media had to work twice as hard to manufacture the illusion that this was a popular leader taking office instead of a usurper imposed by Amazon, Google, Facebook, and the rest of the political, cultural,

---

and economic oligarchy which owns the media on America.

CNN, a subsidiary of AT&T, had already gushed about, "Joe Biden's arms embracing America." MSNBC, a subsidiary of Comcast, compared Biden to God. "He heals the brokenhearted and binds up their wounds." The only wounds being bound up were those of the ruling class which had temporarily lost electoral power to an army of flyover country workers and peasants, only to reclaim it with sedition, wiretapping, abuse of power, billions of dollars, and soldiers in the street…

…Biden isn't a charismatic leader. He isn't moving the cause forward. He's a placeholder for a ruling class that wants homes in Dupont Circle that it buys by selling out America to China, by ruining our economy with environmental consulting gigs and racial contract quotas, and for all the manifold ways which the swamp is coming back as Biden's wetlands restoration project.

"Hail to the Thief" is as much their anthem as it is Biden's. They fought to keep hold of D.C., the center of their power base not because they care about its history or that of this country, but because it's where they network, collaborate, and do their dirty little deals at our expense.

The troops in the street are their warning to the rest of the country about who is really in charge.

At the risk of going off on a tangent, I left the following as a comment on one of the articles I sourced for this morning. That said, it is nevertheless appropriate given some of the completely blind attitudes of some pundits as to how our world has been turned upside down since (s)Election Day:

"We are not voting our way out of this ever again. But the root of the problem was, is and always will be the schools. Yes, the election was stolen and America was overthrown for sure at the ballot box. But that could never have happened had the previous two to three generations of our citizenry not had their minds poisoned from K through post-grad. Anything even remotely socialist in terms of politicians would've been a joke, as it was in 1980 when Gus Hall and Angela Davis ran on the Communist Party line.

But only 29 years later, a man who voted for them became the director of the CIA while his boss, whose father/father-figure was a Stalinist enemy, became President. And here we are 12 years later, in a nightmare that will make 09-16 look like a walk in the park.

Crackpots like Ibram X. Kendi are not outliers; they are mainstream not only in failed urban shit-holes, but in schools all across the country. Unless and until we purge every classroom and lecture hall of his acolytes – who I fear are the majority in academia – we do not stand a snowball's chance in hell. And with virtually every other aspect of our society and government controlled by, beholden to or otherwise cheering on the tyranny, the task may very well be impossible at this point."

And yet, we are still here. Millions and millions of us. I don't have to invite the Enemy to do their worst; you can bet your life that that is exactly what they are going to do. It will be a testament to our character how we respond.

Friday, January 22, 2021

The rollercoaster of emotions are back. After the Enemy stole the election, my mood violently rocked Voyage-to-the-Bottom-of-the-Sea explosion-like, back and forth between hope and despair. Now actually, since the installation ceremony of Josef Visarrionovich Robinette Stolin[112] on Wednesday that made a low grade Triumph of the Will outtake look like the "Broadway Melody" number from Singin' in the Rain, my emotions believe it or not have lifted somewhat — from abject dread to mere depression.

Look, there is no getting around the fact that we are at the mercy not only of Obama's merry band of insane

---

112 Joe Biden.

Maoists, who are now unchained after four years of watching one man – one great American and one of the greatest presidents ever – reverse the disaster of the previous eight years (and more really) that they inflicted on us, and are frothing at the mouth and out for blood. A good deal of that rage is not only the reversal, but the demonstration that every policy position, every social, cultural and political belief were one by one, over the course of the past four years dismantled and demonstrated for all the world to see to be utterly wrong to the point of farcical.

Remember the halcyon days of late 2016 when then-candidate Trump promised to return millions of jobs back to America, an America that Obama and the Democrat Party insisted was in decline (because of their actions) and who actually boasted about his (Obama's) ability to manage the decline and make our national sublimation as painless as possible? Obama asked "what's he gonna do, wave a magic wand?" Well, Trump sure did. It's called free market capitalism, deregulation, low taxes, and tariffs that level the playing field to make free trade fair. Jobs came back in the millions, manufacturing concerns opened new plants, minorities and the poor went off the welfare and food stamp rolls and got to work in astounding, record-breaking numbers. The greatest economic boom was yuuge, luxurious, obvious and to Obama and his globalist cronies, was the equivalent of having the dog poo they soiled the carpet with not only rubbed in their faces, but rammed back up their keisters.

Well, we all know the score since then. So, why do I feel a bit more upbeat, for lack of a better word? Because, despite the fact that virtually every instrumentality of government and political process (I'm looking at the GOP) as well as the media, academia and shockingly more and more of the private sector are in league with what can only be described as a junta, nearly 80 million people did not vote for this, and perhaps another 100 to 150 million who didn't participate in the election want no part of it. With upwards of two thirds of the populace believing that those in power are illegitimate, that is not a recipe for "unity." It's a powder keg. Even if Uncle Joe Stolin[113] was sincere about unity, the only way to unify a country is if the two sides had something in common that was far above policy differences. It's what's known in the trade as a "shared national identity." At least the Union and the Confederacy shared a Judeo-Christian ethic as well as the Constitution, despite the interpretation of the latter being a major factor in a bloody civil war. The Leftists and us normal Americans share nothing in common. They view us, our culture, history and heritage as a cancer to be eradicated. They seek our subjugation or destruction. And that lack of commonality is potentially infinitely more destructive than even that which drove us apart in 1861. Had the Confederacy won, they'd have gained their independence and left the rest of the Union alone, other factors notwithstanding. That is a non-starter with the current junta, its allies, voters and vote forgers.

---

113 Joe Biden

And oddly enough, that is the source of my mood elevation, as such. Given the mood of the population, there is really no room for this junta to make any mistake or overreach, or otherwise further antagonize tens of millions of pissed off people. But given who they are, their arrogance and their *Gott mit uns*[114] attitude means its only a matter of time before they do exactly that. Who had 12 hours? Come get your prize. Nancy Pelosi and Chuck Schumer are evidently starting up not only a completely illegal and unconstitutional post-presidency impeachment of President Trump, they are also attempting to expel and even criminally prosecute members of Congress who objected to the Electoral College results on January 6th, Black Wednesday. And the FBI is now attempting to identify anyone who was in the Capitol building and send them up the river. Insult? Meet Injury! The National Guardsmen who were used as props while at the same time blood-libeled as white supremacists and potential assassins at the inaugural were housed like livestock in a D.C. parking garage before being told to get the hell out of the city so that their odor would not offend the delicate sensibilities of our elites.

I hope every Guardsmen there has a long memory, and is keeping their powder dry.

---

114 https://en.wikipedia.org/wiki/Gott_mit_uns

Monday, January 25, 2021

The start of the first full week under the Enemy junta. It may resemble a Givenchy pump or Testoni loafer, but its hobnail jackboot pedigree is unmistakable. As I said last week at the funeral of what remained of the United States of America, the policy insanity that started on day one wiping out jobs, threatening national security and pimping sexual deviancy will be bad enough. But those who were willing to actually steal an election are now going to use every cubicle in every office in every department in every agency of a feral, all powerful, unstoppable governmental bureaucracy, aided and abetted by media propagandists of the old and newfangled variety to wipe out any and all resistance and voices of opposition from every corner of the land — even if they have to imprison or otherwise ruin the lives of 80 million of us to do so. Or worse.

It's for all the marbles, right here and right now. That low budget "inauguration" saw thousands of National Guardsmen used (and abused) as props of the junta, not to protect a legitimately elected president from some supposed "white supremacist" extremist threat but as an extremely unsubtle show of force to anyone who dares question its legitimacy and authority. Already there are efforts to eject actual political opposition leaders like Josh Hawley and Ted Cruz as well as others in the House for exercising their legal, Constitutional prerogatives in objecting to the Electoral College results. Beyond that, ordinary citizens who worked for, voted for or otherwise openly supported President Trump or voiced their opinion that the election was stolen are being purged from the public square, fired from their jobs or, like Mike Lindell, having their businesses ruined.

This is how freedom dies. Declare some sort of national emergency, use it as an excuse to suspend as much of the Constitution as possible, then seize absolute power and hold on tightly — by the neck (and the wallet, as we shall see) of those you have seized it from. Even before the Chinese Lung AIDS – a virus that has an IFR (infection fatality rate) of about 0.03% – was used as the pretext to destroy our economy and further cripple an already ridiculously easy to cheat voting system, another national crisis was used to severely erode our freedoms, and pave the way for the predicament we're in.

It's rather a bitter irony that the attacks of September 11, 2001, which the Clinton regime could have prevented had it (Jamie Gorelick in particular) not hamstrung our law enforcement and intelligence agencies' abilities to go after real threats from Islamic terrorists as opposed to essentially fictional threats from "anti-government" types and "gun nuts." Even when Bin Laden was being handed to us on a silver platter not once but three times, Clinton refused to take him out. And what did we do to make sure those 3,000 lives did not die in vain? Establish a secret court to give the thinnest veneer of legality to do what had never been done before, spy on our own citizenry, on the pretext of safeguarding our national security. What did the FISA courts do 15 years later? Allow itself to be used as the vehicle by which the DOJ, FBI, CIA and others in power attempted to sabotage the 2016 presidential campaign of Donald Trump. When it was exposed, to the extent that the propaganda wing of the junta allowed it to be in the usual house organs, what did those charged with bringing it to heel and punishing those who abused it do? Not one damned thing.

So, with an election stolen, a fraud installed in the Oval Office (and at least two in the Senate), a Reichstag Fire incident used as the pretext to blood-libel Trump and everyone who supported him and now an illegal post-presidency impeachment move to prevent him from running again as well as a concurrent move to purge his Congressional supporters, I predict that FISA is going to be ramped up and expanded as a tool of what is essentially a neo-Stasi apparatus. The days of "the loyal opposition" are over, my friends. I mean, how can there be a loyal opposition if Trump and his party attempted a violent insurrection on January 6th? (sarcastic).

The junta is now going to move fast and furious (no pun, although…) to purge anyone and anything that dare challenge their authority, on the pretext that to do so is "insurrection." While we're all focused, and rightly so, on the security of our right to bear arms, I would not be surprised if something like Canada's odious, Orwellian "human rights commission" gets fired up on our side of the border as well. I fully expect Mignon "Rump Roast" Clyburn to once again infest the FCC and that Uncle Joe Stolin[115] will deem "net

---

115 Joe Biden

neutrality" as enacted with his crayon and phone. I fully expect, too, that the Supreme Court (packed or not) will not object, that is if anyone dares to file a lawsuit. Worse, the GOP wing of the Democrats led by Pee-Air Defecto[116] will be cheering the loudest.

It might behoove all of us who are registered Republican to change that ASAP, for a couple of reasons which should be eminently clear if you've read this far. Just because I'm paranoid doesn't mean they're not out to get me.

Tuesday, January 26, 2021

And the beat (down) goes on. I'm still numb from everything that's happened since last November, sort of like having my legs amputated at the thigh and yet still feeling like I can run the 100-yard dash. Just one short year ago, which seems like an eternity, Iran was on the ropes like a headless chicken after it's terror mastermind was dispatched, thousands of Hong Kongers were waving the American flag, as well as p-shopped images of Donald Trump's face on the body of Rocky Balboa while singing the Star Spangled Banner, we had virtual full employment while the welfare and food stamp rolls lost millions of formerly lost Democrat souls, we were for the first time in decades the world's leading oil exporter, and every attempt to oust the President – forever my president – or otherwise smear, besmirch or otherwise destroy his voting base failed spectacularly.

---

116 Mitt Romney aka "Pierre Delecto"

Intellectually, I of course fully realize what happened in the intervening year and as noted, particularly since last November. But I just cannot accept it. I will never accept it. And, for lack of a better word, I'm happy about it. To accept what happened from a moral standpoint is almost every bit as reprehensible as those who perpetrated it upon us. I know we each live our own life and have to be concerned with the day-to-day challenges, now about to become exponentially more difficult, of keeping our families fed and with a roof over their heads. What will make it difficult will not only be because of the policy edicts handed down by those pulling the rotting cat-gut marionette strings of Zhou Bai-Din [117] that will put a bullet in the head of the already comatose economy, but more crucially the erosion of our G-d given right to speak freely in protest. It's bad enough when the IRS latches on to you or you get the 3:00AM Paul Manafort treatment from the FBI for some crime real or imagined (but mostly imagined), but it will be infinitely worse when your employers, co-workers, neighbors, the local bank and even your own children turn into Donald Sutherland at the end of Invasion of the Body Snatchers and denounce you for "wrong-think" to your condo board's NKVD/Twitter politruk.

Yeah, I get it. Self-preservation is a thing. Keep your head down, don't talk above a whisper and take your beating. It builds character. There's the makings of an Arbeit Macht Frei-ish slogan for some young Jack Dorsey acolyte to noodle around with. But at some point that cannot stand. There

---

117 Joe Biden

has to be a point where you have much more to gain than you do to lose before you openly, proudly declare you have had enough. It reminds me of the last act in The Longest Yard when Paul Crewe, now ostracized by his teammates who know he's throwing the game for the warden, asks the old guy if it was worth 30 years for belting the warden in the mouth. "To me it was."

What is your freedom worth? Your dignity? Is it better to live on your knees than die on your feet? In many ways small and large, we are going to have to confront ourselves with that question. It was never supposed to be that way. Then again, maybe it was. It is human nature we are dealing with, after all. Big time.

Wednesday, January 27, 2021

It appears as if the illegal and unconstitutional attempt to impeach Donald Trump post-presidency has failed. The reason for the Enemy junta and their co-conspirators in the GOP to do this is not only to humiliate the deposed former President but by successfully convicting and removing him from the elective office that he has not occupied since noon last Wednesday, prevent him from running again in 2024. As if any election going forward is going to be free, fair and not rigged against any challenger to the current junta. Actually, I was kind of looking forward to the trial because, if even for a few weeks, it would keep the Senate busy with bullshit while preventing them from moving forward with the Communist agenda. Not that the Senate or the House even matters at this point since Biden is armed with the extra large Crayola box and putting an "X" on more executive orders in his first week than the past three presidents combined. More importantly, if they did go ahead with this lynching, they'd effectively make a martyr out of President Trump and not only anger two-thirds of the American people (actually 100% of the American people; Democrats have rejected their birthright) but energize an already enraged populist movement.

In any case, impeachment or not, Trump and anyone from the most senior administration official down to the average MAGA hat wearing voter that can be identified is going to be hounded to death. And I mean that quite literally. [118]

> *"The mob that stormed the Capitol on January 6 to try to stop Congress from carrying out its constitutional responsibilities were behaving like domestic enemies of our country. But let's be clear, the John Brennans, Adam Schiffs, and oligarchs in Big Tech who are trying to undermine our constitutionally-protected rights and turn our country into a police state with KGB-style surveillance, are also domestic enemies, and much more powerful, and therefore dangerous, than the mob that stormed the Capitol,"* *[former Congresswoman Tulsi] Gabbard declared...*

---

118 https://pjmedia.com/news-and-politics/tyler-o-neil/2021/01/26/gabbard-sounds-the-alarm-leftists-are-plotting-kgb-style-surveillance-of-conservatives-n1411860

...In remarks last week, Gabbard connected H.R. 350, the Domestic Terrorism Prevention Act of 2021, to the growing demands on the Left that Trump supporters must be "deprogrammed."

"This whole effort, whether you're talking about this bill or people saying that we have to deprogram these Trump cultists and people who voted for Trump because they've been radicalized, all of this just goes to further tear our country apart," Gabbard warned. "And it moves towards the thing Joe Biden said in his inauguration speech that shouldn't happen, which is a dehumanization of your opponent."

She warned that the new domestic "War on Terror" seems to involve identifying conservatives and Trump supporters as dangerous "extremists."

"What characteristics are we looking for as we are building this profile of a potential 'extremist,' what are we talking about? Religious extremists, are we talking about Christians, evangelical Christians, what is a religious extremist? Is it somebody who is pro-life? Where do you take this?" the former congresswoman asked.

I don't know what angle Tulsi Gabbard is playing at, and although she came across in the Democrat primary flea circus of 2019 as a voice of reason, she's still a Democrat. But, aside from her remark about the "mob that stormed the Capitol" which ignores the fact that it was led by Antifa/BLM goons posing as Trump supporters, she is absolutely dead right about who is now leading the purges and the danger it poses. I mean, when you publicly attack John Brennan and Adam Schiff as public enemies posing more of a danger than the Black Wednesday mob, you are painting a target on your forehead. Whatever she's thinking, I applaud her for her statement. The fact that the GOP in unison did not join with her also speaks volumes about the nature of that party.

Thursday, January 28, 2021

I'm not going to lie to you. Things are getting bleaker by the day, and we're only eight days into what is for all intents and purposes an illegal, criminal junta. With the stroke of a few dozen crayons, Joe Stolin[119] has wiped out thousands of jobs with the shuttering of Keystone XL, which will multiply exponentially as the blast wave hits the rest of the economy, ditto for the canceling of drilling and mining permits on public lands, halted the construction of the necessary and effective border wall, and sending what's left of our demoralized and abused men and women, and now Frankenstein monster hermaphrodites and other psychotic freaks and other bitter Klingers who make Dame Edna look like Chesty Puller into various and sundry third world meat grinders for no other reason than to keep Raytheon and TRW stocks

---

119 ibid 46, 49

pumped. Would be fitting if the same Wall Street corporatists and cronies got the Game Stop treatment as well, but I digress.

That and so much more in only one week was the hobnailed jackboot to the groin. *Now comes the stomp on the head. Political persecution and punishment of any and all voices of opposition. Daniel Greenfield at Frontpage Mag:*[120]

> *The difference between resistance and sedition, between protests and insurrections, is who's in charge. Democrats resist Republican elected officials. Republicans however commit sedition against Democrat elected officials. Democrats protest, Republicans riot. These aren't distinctions in law. The only real distinction is who's in power and who's on the barricades.*
>
> *Political hypocrisy isn't a new phenomenon, but Democrats weaponizing the national security state to suppress the political opposition over the same behavior they engage in is a serious threat to the survival of the United States as anything other than a banana republic in a civil war.*
>
> *The Democrats fired the first shot when the Obama administration used the national security system to target members of Congress during its time in office and then, in an election year, went after President*

---

120 https://www.frontpagemag.com/fpm/2021/01/when-resistance-became-sedition-and-sedition-daniel-greenfield/

Trump's associates based on Hillary Clinton's opposition research.

Instead of being held accountable for abusing national security to target their political opponents, Democrats, their media, and their allies in the system doubled down with fake investigations of the same worthless allegations that they never managed to substantiate.

After four years of falsely claiming that President Trump was a Russian agent and that the 2016 election had somehow been rigged with Facebook ads in an event that was worse than 9/11, the Democrats have pivoted to claiming that questioning the 2020 election is worse than 9/11.

Now the old abuse of the national security state under the guise of hunting down the evidence that Republicans had rigged the 2016 election has turned into abusing the national security state to punish Republicans for suggesting that the Democrats had rigged the 2020 election.

The only consistent thing here is the Democrat abuse of national security to target their political opponents while magically transforming election skepticism from the highest form of patriotism to sedition, and riots from a moral crusade into a major threat because they are now in power.

Well, you can't have a Great Reset without an even greater deprogramming of wrong-think. Victor Davis Hanson in American Greatness:[121]

> *Retired General Stanley McChrystal warns that the Trump movement reminds him of the al-Qaeda terrorists who once flocked to a similar "powerful leader" – presumably Osama bin Laden.*
>
> *Indeed, our retired military, once critical of the use of the military as domestic police, had no objection to deploying nearly 30,000 soldiers on Inauguration Day in the capital – all on the lookout for nests of Trump insurrectionists.*
>
> *So Pentagon budgets perhaps should readapt to this reality. What good are missiles and jets when NRA members with MAGA hats roam freely in our midst?*
>
> *To help McChrystal and Austin, we could enlist former CIA director John Brennan, former FBI Director James Comey, and former DNI director James Clapper to form a Deprogramming Task Force to root out the "enemies within."*

---

121   https://amgreatness.com/2021/01/27/how-to-deprogram-us/

Public spirited administration appointees – working closely with Silicon Valley, Wall Street, Hollywood, and New York media elites – might issue lists of all social media users indulging in "hate speech" and "big lies."

As both of these great writers note, much of the apparatus of "deprogramming" America in service to its "fundamental transformation" ramped up, starting with Obama. In truth, the real deprogramming took place over the course of the past 50 or more years in our schools, where two to three generations of American children were brainwashed into hating their country, society, culture and parents. Now, they are in every corporate boardroom, factory floor, business, union hall, military unit, police force and of course classroom across the country.

If you want to call it a ray of hope, the confusion over the impeachment and removal from office of Donald Trump, who has already been removed from office, evidently is going to go forward. Chuck Schumer is clucking his blasphemous chicken lips in lowlife Brooklynese that the trial will go forward. Ultimately though, aside from the five scum traitors on the GOP-wing side of the Senate, there will not be nearly enough votes to reach the two-thirds majority to convict.

No matter, it's all for show. When they go after Trump – in or out of office – they are going after you. Let them. Go ahead Schumer. Turn Donald Trump into Nelson Mandela, Mahatma Gandhi or more appropriately Natan Scharansky and Andrei Sakharov. Do that and you stoke a fire that is ultimately going to consume you and your ilk.

That fire is going to be something to see. Let it burn. Make it burn. Until then, the beatings will continue until morale improves.

Friday, January 29, 2021

While the big story is the little guys breaking the rigged casino in the GameStop/Robinhood saga, there are other things going on of equal importance that are probably not going to be getting the attention they deserve. Beyond the schadenfreude of watching actual vulture capitalists get taken down as well as the rage-inducing actions of the junta and its cronies rushing in to illegally shut down thousands of ordinary folks to protect the racket while at the same time threatening to go after those same ordinary folks for merely beating the house by playing the game by its own rules (sound familiar?), there are these items that came over the transom within the past 12 hours as I was aggregating the links:

Democrat Lawmakers Introduce Bill for Nationwide Mail-in Voting: Necessary to "Make Real Progress"[122]

The bill, introduced by Sen. Ron Wyden (D-OR) and Rep. Earl Blumenauer (D-OR), is designed to "fight voter suppression" as detailed by Wyden's press release.

122 https://www.breitbart.com/politics/2021/01/28/democrat-lawmakers-introduce-bill-nationwide-mailin-voting-necessary-make-real-progress/

The measure would "massively expand vote-at-home ballot access, provide voters with pre-paid ballot envelopes and enact automatic voter registration"...

... The lawmakers point to the unprecedented number of Americans who voted by mail in the 2020 presidential election — a move Democrats vehemently pushed. While progressives largely used the coronavirus pandemic as justification for opening the doors for mass mail-in voting, which many critics warn leads to mass fraud, universal vote-by-mail has existed as a primary goal for the Democrat Party, even prior to the pandemic. **The measure introduced on Thursday essentially updates the vote-by-mail measure the two lawmakers introduced in 2017, long before the Wuhan virus struck.**

Emphasis mine. Number two on the hit parade:

Senate Judiciary Chairman Says Gun Control Is "Top Priority"[123]

"Today I had the chance to speak with a group of gun violence prevention advocates from across the country," Durbin tweeted. "I told them that reducing gun violence will be a top priority of the Senate

---

123 https://freebeacon.com/democrats/senate-judiciary-chairman-says-gun-control-is-top-priority/

Judiciary Committee. And I will never stop fighting for gun safety."

Democrats enjoy a slim majority in the Senate with Vice President Kamala Harris able to cast tie-break-ing votes, a partisan split that makes sweeping, new gun-control legislation difficult to pass. Durbin's control of the Judiciary Committee, however, will allow him to shape America's legal landscape. His ability to shepherd President Joe Biden's judicial nominees to federal courts could play a decisive role in numerous gun-rights cases. The committee also oversees federal law that regulates firearms, including the federal gun background check system.

Sen. Chuck Grassley (R., Iowa), the committee's top Republican, said he hopes Durbin will pursue similar gun initiatives to the past Congress instead of attempting to push through sweeping liberal changes.

*"Unduly abridging or regulating those rights, espe-cially if it's through a strictly partisan process, is wrong," Grassley told the Washington Free Beacon. "**I hope, if Senator Durbin chooses to focus on this issue, it will be with a bipartisan, consensus-building approach.**"*

Again, emphasis mine. Yes, once again, if we're going to disarm private citizens let's make sure we preserve a fig leaf of an illusion of a fairy tale that it's completely kosher. Chuck Grassley is a fossil and a fraud. Then again, it's not as if regular order means anything anymore. And with the courts about to be packed so tight Roman Polanski will wrestle Biden to see who can marry it, at least 100 million people now labeled as insurrectionist will be reclassified as armed terrorists. As an aside, Nancy Pelosi bitching about Rep. Lauren Boebert carrying in the halls of Congress is quite rich considering she (Pelosi) was supposedly fearing for her life because of the "rioters."

Finally, John Kerry, a man who made his fortune the old fashioned way, by shacking up with wealthy broads impressed with his phony Crackerjack box medals, farted out this little gem:

Climate Czar John Kerry Says Tens of Thousands of Jobs Will Be Cut for Zero Benefit[124]

> *"He [Biden] knows [the] Paris [Accord target] alone is not enough. Not when almost 90% of all of the planet's emissions, global emissions come from outside of U.S. borders. We could go to zero tomorrow and the problem isn't solved."*

Beyond the obvious problems of using low-density energy sources like wind and solar to power high-density living in urban and suburban areas, the assertions the admin-

---

124 https://pjmedia.com/news-and-politics/stacey-lennox/2021/01/28/climate-czar-john-kerry-says-tens-of-thousands-of-jobs-will-be-cut-for-zero-benefit-n1416710

istration is making about workforce opportunities and even U.S. manufacturing are absurd. We are going to kill millions of jobs for absolutely nothing. Canceling the Keystone XL project was a gift to Vladimir Putin and his petrol economy, just as no new leases on federal land will be. Pushing a rapid transition to green will be a boon for the Chinese Communist Party while they continue to pollute at alarming rates and lie about it.

Welcome back to leading from behind, only worse. Climate Czar John Kerry, who has gotten almost nothing right in his entire career, will drag the economy down with him this time. After all, not everyone can marry a ketchup heiress.

Emphasis mine. Add these items to the elimination of our borders and amnesty for upwards of 30 million illegal aliens already here, the move to once again prop up the mad Muslim mullahs in Iran and let them build an A-bomb – which will touch off a war in the Gulf, the aiding and abetting of the Chi-Coms to seize global economic and geo-political domination, and the ramping up of political persecution and repression here in the former United States of America and we are looking at a situation, folks.

The reality is, even if we had a political party to try and fight this – which we do not – there is nothing they can do to prevent or even slow down any of this. The Grassley attitude of "if I'm going to get gang-raped by AIDS-infected chimpanzees, at least they better take me to dinner first" is fully on display. If anyone thinks that 2022 and 2024 are going to make any difference whatsoever, they're delusional. I guess it comes full circle back to l'affaire GameStop. While the system may very well have always been rigged, Donald J. Trump came along in 2016 and in essence "beat the house." And for four years, he singlehandedly exposed those who are back in power now as the frauds, poseurs and incompetents that they were, just by enacting policies that made Americans more prosperous, more secure and more free than at any time since the end of the Second World War — which not coincidentally was when the malignant cancer of Globalism first metastasized.

So, what can we do? For starters, I would say while you still have the opportunity arm yourself to the teeth. Start developing and strengthening social ties with family and friends who you know have the same political bent and can be trusted, and figure out how to communicate in a way that is as private as you can make it. It would be nice if red states went the full on nullification route, if not secession. The states where Keystone XL runs should tell Biden to go fuck himself and build the damn pipeline anyway.

I think for the first time, thanks to the actions of this illegal, criminal junta, a very large swath of the citizenry are going to face a situation where, stripped of an income and perhaps facing serious economic hardship will collectively have nothing to lose. I hope and pray that it never comes to this, but to not see the signposts that this is indeed the direction we are headed is to be blind.

Those in power right now are not only playing with matches, but they're doing so inside of a gasoline refinery. Pun intended.

Monday, February 1, 2021

February. Already? Before marveling at the speed that time seems to be passing, a mere scanning of the headlines shows the next four to eight years are going to be interminable. And I say "four to eight years" advisedly since it presumes normal free and fair elections, which flies in the face of my declaration that the United States of America ceases to exist; its demise the result of the theft of the 2020 national election.

In the lead is the news that Lincoln Project cofounder John Weaver is not a poor, put upon closeted gay man who was wrenched from his hiding place by cruel, bigoted Trump-supporting Bible-thumpers, but a chronically sick pedophile who had been luring and abusing young boys — for years. However miserable bastards like Bill Kristol, Steve Schmidt and Rick Wilson try to spin this and distance themselves from Weaver, it turns out that none other than fellow fat failure and Trump-hater Karl Rove blew the whistle on Weaver way back in 2004. The accusation came out in lefty house organ The Atlantic which, in the failed effort to drag John Kerry across the finish line, was bashing anyone associated with Dubya, instead of doing real journalism. Shocking, I know.

Aside from the schadenfreude of watching a leading Never-Trumper and traitor to the former republic squirm, my first reaction is big deal; the Enemy and its propagandists will either use the news to bash the GOP, itself a sham organization used to perpetuate the illusion of opposition and keep us subjugated without real political power, or they'll bury it in the next news cycle, since the Lincoln Project is a useful ally (for the moment) to the junta. The latter needs the former to transmit the meme that Trump, Trumpism, the MAGA agenda and all they collectively represent are responsible for the riots, division and suffering of 2020 – which the Enemy alone was responsible for – as well as the blame for the suffering and destruction that's to come, and will doubtless make 2020 look like Salad Days.

Again, I don't have to tell you the score; it's bleak, depressing and downright frightening. And two of my favorite writers/pundits, kind of irritated me a bit today. First, Daniel Greenfield was all bent of shape over Rep. Marjorie Taylor Greene.[125]

> *Instead of talking about Biden's barrage of unconstitutional executive orders, about his radical appointees, and about what Schumer and Pelosi are plotting to do with our country, we're talking about Greene's kooky idea that Jewish space lasers are starting forest fires.*

---

125 https://www.frontpagemag.com/fpm/2021/02/kooks-marjorie-taylor-greene-sabotage-our-fight-daniel-greenfield-editors/

Or we're discussing her 9/11 Truther nonsense or her school shooting conspiracy theories.

Greene's laser nonsense has been condemned by conservative Jewish groups from the Coalition for Jewish Values to the Republican Jewish Coalition. Her presence in the Republican Party undermines our fight against Democrat leftist anti-Semitic racists like Rep. Ilhan Omar.

The Democrat Party is the party for anti-Semitic kooks. It's the party for nuts who think Bush flew the planes into the World Trade Center and that kids murdered in schools by violent thugs were really actors. We don't need this garbage and right now we can't afford the distraction.

Okay, yeah, I get it. She's a chucklehead that does us no favors by opening her yap. But the fact is the Enemy already controls the media and are going to bash her as hard as they are ripping into people like Josh Hawley and Ted Cruz, whom they are a red nether hair's breadth away for charging with treason and then hanging. This is a political party and movement that has packed Congress as well as dozens of state and local governments with rabid racialists, anti-Semites and bust-out Marxists from top to bottom. Hell, the DNC's platform comprises all of that as openly as BLM declares itself to be Marxist. Frankly, I'm more concerned with getting rid of the likes of Mitt Romney, Liz Cheney and the Chamber of Commerce than making Marjorie Taylor Greene the focus of my efforts.

Tuesday, February 2, 2021

Speaking of overthrowing governments and sabotaging elections, the legally elected government in Myanmar was overthrown by a military coup over, get this, "suspected election fraud." The image up top is evidently an aerobics instructor doing her routine while the military was caught in the background rolling into the parliament to arrest – yet again – Aung San Suu Kyi. Can't wait for Jen Psaki to "psircle" back on this one. Feh. The ease with which the firewalls protecting our freedoms and our rights were blown away have not been lost on the enemy junta; in fact, while fear porn of allegedly even more virulent strains of this Chinese virus continue to be pimped and pumped in the junta's house organs, the reaction to the other phony crisis, so-called "climate change" is going to make what was done to us this past year seem like nothing. With no courts and no political party to stop this – indeed with any vocal opposition at all to be deemed as "hate speech" or "insurrectionist," (and those are sure to be codified and rubber-stamped as the law of the land very soon now), well, you get the picture. Yet, the Enemy are saying and doing things that strike me and others as more out of fear than confidence.[126]

---

126 https://www.americanthinker.com/articles/2021/02/the_tells_of_the_deep_state_poker_players.html

Why would [quote-unquote so-called] President Biden shovel out a boatload of executive orders in the first week of his presidency advancing climate change and fighting systemic racism?

Why would the Deep State sic the FBI on a candidate and then President Trump, and then let Kevin Cline-smith, the guy that falsified a document, off with a tap on the wrist?

Why would the rulers nod and wink through a summer of riots that caused death and destruction in many American cities, and then build fences and call out the National Guard to protect them against a few "far-right" LARPers? And if that isn't enough, mount an impeachment against a president who has already left office?

Oh, and by the way, how come it was Vice President Pence that ordered up the National Guard to Washington D.C.? Why not Trump, the commander-in-chief? Inquiring minds would like to know.

What is going on here? These "tells" show that the ruling class, for all its power and its domination and hegemony, is terrified by the barbarians at the gates.

They've got the power and they're going to use it. And the more things fail, the more some people speak out and act, to the extent they will be allowed, the more the junta is going to crack down and double down. They hate us, and they fear us.[127]

> *...Democracy can be a wondrous thing and it is certainly a desirable thing, but it can also be the tyranny of the majority. Democracy can be self-defeating, as a tyrannical majority or vanguard party can elect a despot or vote to undo democracy (the Bolshevik Revolution comes to mind), but today its chief opponents are not the populists but the elites...*
>
> *The establishment spent the past four years panicking, not that a demagogue might undo democracy in the West but that a Republican might remind the West that it is democratic. No, President Trump did not injure or hurt democracy. He simply reminded the establishment that democracy was still the expectation — that even in a republic the citizens are in control. Democracy has not been beaten by the populist movement. It was resuscitated. In fact, it was the elites who were given cause to fret. Why? Western peoples have begun to see all that they share in common with one another extra to common sense; that they have been pitted against one another so that they may remain blind to their real foe: to the unac-*

---

127 https://amgreatness.com/2021/02/01/the-democratic-injury-davos-against-a-free-west/

countable elite who wage a never-ending rebellion against the poor and against normalcy.

"It is the mark of our whole modern history that the masses are kept quiet with a fight," wrote [G.K.] Chesterton. "They are kept quiet by the fight because it is a sham-fight; thus most of us know by this time that the Party System has been popular only in the sense that a football match is popular."

Americans and Britons and other Westerners are tired of this game where, regardless of the score, they are losing. Leyen, Merkel, Macron, et al. are right to panic, for democratic peoples may soon be willing to fight a real fight and for keeps.

Perhaps there is, if not a solution then a way to stave off and lessen the damage of the rapidly growing totalitarian tyranny American style that is about to engulf us.[128]

In reality, nullification (which I've been advocating for years) should have been pursued long ago; the federal government has, after all, been trampling states' powers for at least the better part of a century, and an ounce of prevention is worth a pound of cure. But that being water under the bridge, we now require a ton of cure.

---

128 https://www.americanthinker.com/articles/2021/02/the_fight_that_lies_between_status_quo_and_secession.html

The cure of nullification is the obvious next step for anyone serious about combating the burgeoning leftist tyranny. We've no other recourse. "As Jefferson warned, if the federal government is allowed to hold a monopoly on determining the extent of its own powers, we have no right to be surprised when it keeps discovering new ones," wrote author Thomas E. Woods, Jr.

Under this scenario, the federal government "will continue to grow — regardless of elections, the separation of powers, and other much-touted limits on government power," he continued.

That is reality. So is this: Reasoned argumentation only works with those who'll yield to reason (the left won't). Constitutional constraints only matter to those who respect laws and national contracts (the left doesn't). Appealing to courts only bears fruit when judges have a sense of justice and duty and the guts to act rightly even when pariah status results (most don't). Making this more tragically comical still is that when we seek redress for federal tyranny, we expect relief from the federal government's own judicial branch!

This didn't help us with the 2020 election, which the left got away with stealing. Moreover, it knows it can not only replicate the theft in the future but can expand it; thus have the Democrats introduced a bill taking mail-in voting nationwide. Perhaps they can pass it, too.

Wednesday, February 3, 2021

The big story is President-in-exile Donald Trump's second "impeachment" trial. On the face of it, it's an absolute farce; Trump cannot be subject to a process the sole purpose of which is to remove him from an elected office that he no longer occupies. If one needs to go beyond that, the "charges" against him are completely baseless, without merit, and defy the timeline of events that occurred on Black Wednesday, January 6.

Just off the top of my head, these are the events as I have seen, heard and read about from multiple, reliable eyewitness sources:

1. The overwhelming majority of rally-goers on January 6 were no doubt fired up and passionate about showing up as a way of registering their displeasure at Congress and VP Pence giving the Good Housekeeping seal of approval to the Electoral College vote.

2. In calling for his supporters to come to D.C., at no time did President Trump demand, encourage, promote nor even hint at anyone "getting in the

faces" of elected officials or being in any way, shape or form destructive.

3. D.C. Mayor Muriel Bowser and other Democrat elected officials knew in advance that there would be trouble and yet did not call for reinforcements nor did they take any other precautions. There is ample reason to suspect that she and the echelons of the D.C. cops as well as high level Democrats colluded with Antifa/BLM agitators in advance to stage Reichstag Fire 2: Electric Boogaloo.

4. The actual breaching of the Capitol buildings were led by Antifa/BLM confederates dressed in MAGA gear and in fact were shown to be let in and guided by Capitol Police. It is they who caused whatever minimal damages to property that occurred. John Sullivan, a rabid racialist BLM-tifa leader called for burning the place down on social media whist wearing a MAGA hat and Palestinian terror towel around his neck. Those few dozen who followed them in were seen to be behaving as if they were on a guided tour instead of the mostly peaceful Democrat arsonists who torched a dozen cities over the course of the summer and afterwards.

5. 5The breach occurred on or about the time Trump started speaking, so he could not have ordered the storming of the Bastille as it was already well under way. Plus, any honest analysis of what he

said will show at no time did he tell people to storm Congress or act in any way, shape or form that could be remotely construed as violent.

6. Ashli Babbitt was shot in cold blood by a Capitol cop and, surprise, surprise, no reasonable prosecutor will hold the killer to account. One has to wonder beyond the actions and mindset of the assassin what would be revealed about his higher ups regarding preparations for that day. But that's just conspiracy talk, right? The others who sadly died that day evidently were not as a result of any violent confrontation.

7. When he learned of what was going on in Congress, Trump himself told everyone to disperse and go home as quickly, quietly and peacefully as possible.

8. "Bomb planted at the RNC headquarters the night before? Never heard of it!" — Charlie Gibson

Thursday, February 4, 2021

I don't know how much more of this upside down, Orwellian, Kafkaesque nightmare I can stomach. It all boils down to one thing: It's the hypocrisy, stupid. One of the leaders of this creeping blob of cancer is Chuck Schumer, a man (on paper) who has never done an honest hour's, let alone day's work in his miserable existence. Of all the shrill, shrieking, screeching megaphones of malevolence, his lowlife, nasal Flatbush accent is among the loudest and most detestable in its hypocrisy. Mollie Hemingway lets him have it at The Federalist:[129]

Less than one year ago, Sen. Chuck Schumer of New York led a mob on the steps of the Supreme Court while a case was being heard and tried to thwart the natural deliberation of justices by violently threatening two of them to rule in favor of his and other Democrats' preferred outcome.

"I want to tell you, Gorsuch, I want to tell you, Kavanaugh, you have released the whirlwind, and you will pay the price. You won't know what hit you if you go forward with these awful decisions," Schumer threatened the two most recently confirmed justices, Neil Gorsuch and Brett Kavanaugh.

The threat was so alarming that even leftist activists such as Laurence Tribe condemned it. Schumer received a rare, same-day rebuke from Chief Justice John Roberts, who said, "Justices know that criticism comes with the territory, but threatening statements of this sort from the highest levels of government are not only inappropriate, they are dangerous..."

---

129 https://thefederalist.com/2021/02/03/chuck-schumer-used-violent-rhetoric-to-sic-a-mob-on-two-supreme-court-justices/

... Schumer's threats came just 17 months after the Supreme Court had been besieged and attacked by abortion activists upset at Kavanaugh's confirmation. Like the Jan. 6 event, the October 2018 siege also involved Vice President Mike Pence being condemned by protesters. As he walked down the steps of the U.S. Senate following the vote to confirm Kavanaugh, the crowd greeted him with chants of "shame!"

Across the street, hordes of protesters broke through a police barricade and attempted to beat down the 13-ton bronze doors of the court. Protesters included a topless woman with a Hitler mustache and another woman who scaled the Contemplation of Justice statue in front of the court and sat in her lap to the cheers of other protesters...

... Democrats' argument in favor of Trump's impeachment is that even though he told his protesters to be peaceful, his refusal to accept the 2020 election incited a mob. What to do, then, with a Senate majority leader who issued a violent threat against Supreme Court justices after a multi-year campaign to undermine confidence in Supreme Court confirmation processes?

Chuck Schumer is a clown in the way that that little corporal with the Charlie Chaplin mustache, was a clown.

He may not be a great speechmaker, but when you have the power of the State behind you, the trains will run on time just the same. Not him personally, of course, but an alarming number of people who voted for President Joe Aqualung[130] that are up your street and in some cases living under the same roof as you. How did this happen? Slowly, then all at once.[131]

Friday, February 5, 2021

Near the top [of the headlines] is the House voting to strip Marjorie Taylor Greene of her committee assignments, with 11 useless sods from the GOP wing of the Democrats crossing the aisle to stab one of the few honest, open voices of dissent remaining in Congress in the heart, or in her case, the throat. I'll say this up front – I could care less about what Greene allegedly said regarding so-called "conspiracy theories" and whatnot. The fact is she is a staunch supporter of our deposed President-in-Exile Trump and by extension the American people. Given the fact that the Democrats continue to smear her and all of us as "insurrectionist" for daring to even question the legitimacy of what was clearly a hijacked election makes me stand by Rep. Greene that much more staunchly. Beyond that, as has been pointed out here and elsewhere, the fact that the entirety of the Democrat congressional contingent and the majority of its GOP wing

130 Joe Biden

131 https://amgreatness.com/2021/02/03/when-centrism-becomes-extremism/

include vermin such as Eric Swalwell and are praised and elevated as great Americans despite knowingly or otherwise cavorting and consorting with Red Chinese agents, among other things, makes the persecution of Greene that much more loathsome and detestable. Then again, the fact that the government as a whole is indeed an illegitimate junta that has about as much regard for the Constitution as I do for dog turd on the bottom of my shoe, Greene's removal from committees are a meaningless gesture from a practical legislative standpoint. Indeed, if she plays her cards and the media right (and there's no guarantee she can), the Dems would have made a blunder in not following Vito Corleone's advice of "keep your friends close but your enemies closer."

All that brings me to the related and more important story of Bank of America now actively and eagerly working with the FBI to hunt down and persecute anyone who was in or even near the Capitol on Black Wednesday. This development is absolutely bone-chilling in its implications.[132]

> *What we've witnessed in the last 20 or so years is a fusion between big corporations, from big tech on down, and the federal government. Both institutions have complete fealty to a Democrat-run state and will do all in their power to preserve it.*
>
> *…Once upon a time, only the government was powerful enough to censor people and it was only the*

---

132 https://www.americanthinker.com/blog/2021/02/bank_of_america_is_working_with_the_fbi_to_hunt_down_trump_supporters.html

state that had the criminal laws and police power that made illegal searches an issue. Now, though, corporations have taken over the public squares in which speech once took place and they possess every bit of private information we own.

Because the corporations and the federal government share common values (after all, they all went to the same colleges and were taught the same way of thinking), they are tag-teaming: The Democrat-run bureaucracy, White House and Congress, express an unconstitutional desire and the corporations fill it without implicating that hoary old document.

And that gets me to Tucker Carlson's report on Thursday night.[133] It turns out that Bank of America voluntarily got on the computer and searched its databases — that means, it searched your private financial records — to learn whether you traveled to D.C., stayed anywhere within a vast radius of D.C., bought anything at a weapons store in D.C. (whether ammo or a can opener), and bought airline tickets to anywhere.

If, or perhaps when we abolish cash and institute digital currency, anything and everything you purchase will be compiled, indexed, filed, numbered, referenced and cross-

---

133 https://dailycaller.com/2021/02/04/tucker-carlson-bank-of-america-purchase-capitol-riot-investigation/

referenced for anything "troubling." Not just cigarettes, booze or even porn. But firearms, ammo, an American flag, a contribution to B'nai Brith, a subscription to the Limbaugh Letter, hitting the AOS or CJN tip jar etc. etc. And when you want to buy a house, a car or health insurance (assuming it's still allowed) you might get a little note from some apparatchik stating you have to turn over all your weapons since "owning firearms is dangerous to your health."

This is what happens when two to three generations of our children are brainwashed all day and every day from kindergarten through post-graduate. You don't need a Secret Police when potentially anyone including your own family members will do that job for free in order to "stop white supremacy" or "save the planet."

C.S. Lewis nailed it:

> *"Of all the tyrannies, a tyranny sincerely exercised for the good of its victims may be the most oppressive. It may be better to live under robber barons than under the omnipotent moral busybodies. The robber barons cruelty may sometimes sleep, his cupidity may at some point be satiated; but those who torment us for our own good will torment us without end, for they do so with the approval of their own conscience."*

Monday, February 8, 2021

To paraphrase the noxious emissions from Ilhan Omar, congratulations to some people for doing something yesterday. I understand it remotely resembled what was our most popular sporting event that long ago almost the entire nation watched, and in so doing for at least one weekend a year bridged all socio-economic, cultural and political divides. But since we no longer have a nation, and since sports like virtually every other aspect of our culture and heritage has now become weaponized as an instrument in service to our repression, yesterday's pseudo-event, as Marshal McLuhan would describe it, is meaningless. It's Rollerball without the pocket-sized flamethrower, groovy 70s costumes and Bach's Toccata and Fugue in D Minor.

Instead of misplacing the 13th century ("Not much in the century, just Dante and a few corrupt Popes, but it's so distracting and annoying!")[134], we're on the precipice of repeating the first half of the 20th and "misplacing" with extreme prejudice, every real aspect of human and societal progress in the truest sense of that abused word since Magna Carta.[135]

The point of the 1960s, again we were taught, was to tear down the rules, the traditions and customs, the hierarchies of the old guys. The targets were sup-

---

134 https://www.imdb.com/title/tt0073631/characters/nm0724732

135 https://amgreatness.com/2021/02/07/our-animal-farm/

posedly the uptight, short-hair, square-tie, adult gen-eration who grew up in the Depression, won World War II, and were fighting to defeat Cold War Soviet Union.

The good guys, the students, and the activists, if they only had power, were going to break up corpora-tions, shame (or "eat") the rich, and bring in young, hip politicians. Reformers like the younger Kennedy brothers, the John Kerry war hero-resisters, the Bay Area Dianne Feinsteins, and the hip Nancy Pelosis would disrupt the "status quo" of politics.

They would all push hard for assimilation and inte-gration of the races, and the equality of the sexes in pursuit of universal equality of opportunity. The mantra of the 1960s and 1970s was "opportunity." Remember the 1964 federal EEOC — the Equal Employment Opportunity Commission…

…Fast forward a half-century. What did these now-late septuagenarians give America?

We are now finally witnessing the logical fruition of their radical utopia: Censorship, electronic surveil-lance, internal spying, monopolies, cartels, conspiracy theories, weaponization of the intelligence agencies, pouring billions of dollars into campaigns, changing voting laws by fiat, a woke revolutionary military, book banning, bleeding the First Amendment, canceling careers, blacklisting, separate-but-equal racial segregation and separatism...

...The revolutionary animals are now running the farm in a way that would be nightmarish even to Farmer Jones.

Wednesday, February 10, 2021

The farcical debasement of the rule of law and any semblance of justice, political comity and fairness that were (or what we chose to believe) the hallmarks of the American way is the top story. And honestly, I could not really care less about it. About the only useful things yesterday's proceedings demonstrated were the complete immorality and criminality of the Democrat-run junta and yet more confirmation in the form of the six GOP Senators who voted to declare this sham kosher as confederates of the aforementioned tyrants now ruling the nation (for lack of a better word).

Merkin-pated louse Jamie Raskin farting out all he likes about how impeaching a private citizen and removing him from an office he no longer holds is completely constitutional does not and never will make it so. Add into the mix the doctored tapes of the "riot," the omission of PIEOTUS[136] Trump's own words, which never once urged anyone to be anything but peaceful and respectful, and the fact that the foul fossilized Patrick Leahy is acting as both the judge and

---

136 President in Exile of the United States

a key prosecutor in the trial and the whole thing just reeks to high heaven. Well, congratulations fools; you're about to turn Donald Trump into a cross between Mahatma Gandhi and Nelson Mandela to about 200 million very angry people. And that anger will blossom into a taste for vengeance once energy is no longer cheap, work no longer available, food no longer plentiful, and our mouths rhetorically (or otherwise) wired shut to silence our displeasure.

All of this is also sadly revelatory about where we are as a society. The last vestiges of America as founded were mortally wounded on the night of November 3, finished off on January 6 and cremated on January 20. We're now at the salting-of-the-earth-where-it-once-stood-phase, not only with this but with the purging from the public square anyone and anything that dares oppose our subjugation at the hands of the globalists and ultimately the Red Chinese.

On that score, one of the more troubling actions is the complete purging of the military on the pretext of weeding out so-called "white supremacists" in the ranks. Translation, anyone who would swear allegiance to the Constitution of the nation formerly known as the United States of America and refuse to carry out any order that contravenes the letter and spirit of that document.[137]

One of Defense Secretary Lloyd Austin's first actions after confirmation has been to order a "60 day stand down" to combat extremism. This follows the widespread and mostly baseless establishment fantasy that

137 https://amgreatness.com/2021/02/09/the-coming-military-purge/

"right-wing extremists" and "white supremacists" are running rampant and pose some immediate threat to the country.

The details and definitions will ultimately determine whether this campaign is a sensible one that is in keeping with the Constitution or ends up being a purge of the overwhelmingly conservative ranks of the military. No reasonable person would object to removing dangerous and disloyal people from the service, but such a limited goal is distinct from punishing those with merely dissenting and idiosyncratic views. For example, a recent briefing among the Army's Special Forces singled out Pepe the Frog and the Gadsden Flag as signs of extremism. These popular symbols — one a historical American flag — are widely embraced among the mainstream Right...

... Rural, white, conservative, and Christian American men make up the bulk of America's warrior class. They predominate in dangerous combat units, and intergenerational traditions of service are common. In spite of these traditions, the message from the culture, as well as political leaders, to such people is plain: Your day is done. You will be second-class citizens. And you are suspect.

What will happen to the American military if this warrior class chooses not to serve a political regime that labels them obstacles to the goals of equity and inclusion? What will motivate them if such service becomes morally ambiguous and less supported within their own communities?...

...While all the talk of a "coming civil war" is frequently overwrought, it is undeniable that the country is wracked by partisan disagreements, and that the party in power has stated rather explicitly that it believes it is facing some kind of insurgency.

The most elementary principle of counterinsurgency is that force alone cannot succeed. A government under pressure must address the grievances of the insurgents and their communities — i.e., win "hearts and minds." Tightening the screws as hard as possible ends up being counterproductive, as regime overreach creates new insurgents motivated by a combination of revenge and hopelessness.

An increasingly hostile ruling class, who conceive of themselves as occupying a disloyal, irredentist America, is, unfortunately, a formula for weakness abroad and conflict at home.

This is perhaps one of the more frightening developments since the rigged election and the overthrow of the government. And that's saying something because every single part of the massive Leviathan that controls our lives is being dismantled, rejiggered and put on steroids. Now that said, it seems to me that the Marxist junta is in a real pickle with this. On one hand, the old guard greedy power mad goons like Malig-Nancy Pelosi as well as the GOP-e warmongers like Liz-Ard Cheney are in bed with the military industrial complex; they need endless wars to keep the defense contractors in the chips and donating on K-Street. But on the other, the hardcore full-on freaks of the Code Pinko set have a traditional hate on for anything and everything military.

So, if the ranks are purged of experienced and competent soldiers and officers, there still aren't enough transexual freaks looking for a headline or Shillsbury Doughboy Vindmans[138] to take their place. Will it be the Democrats who push for a draft? That would be hilarious, were I not right now weeping for the nation formerly known as the USA.

As far as the seeds of an anti-regime insurrectionist army, there are already 200 million citizens armed with two to three times as many firearms and who knows how much ammunition. I think that that is what keeps the Enemy junta up at night. If a cadre of purged officers like Mike Flynn were ever able to organize even a fraction of that number… I think I just gave myself a stiffie.

*　*　*　*　*

---

138   Lt. Col. Alexander Vindman

AFTERWORD

And the Beat Down Goes On

"Of all the tyrannies, a tyranny sincerely exercised for the good of its victims may be the most oppressive. It may be better to live under robber barons than under the omnipotent moral busybodies. The robber barons cruelty may sometimes sleep, his cupidity may at some point be satiated; but those who torment us for our own good will torment us without end, for they do so with the approval of their own conscience."

– C.S. Lewis

To mark the first 100 days of his new "administration," *Joe Biden, who was pimped as the man who would unite America,* delivered with crystal clarity an unambiguous message of power, lies and fear, all rolled into one overarching theme: Hatred. Hatred of you, me and the nation formerly known as the United States of America.

The tone was set early with a whopper that would have made another famous leftist, Josef Goebbels, beam with pride. Joe Biden referred to the Capitol Hill protest of January 6, 2021, as the... [139]

---

139 https://www.breitbart.com/politics/2021/04/28/fact-check-biden-calls-capitol-riot-worst-attack-on-our-democracy-since-the-civil-war/

"...worst attack on our democracy since the Civil War."

Aside from the fact that we are not a democracy but a representative constitutional republic – or at least we used to be – the absolute ludicrousness of that statement would be laughable were it not for the fact that a large percentage of our population think 9/11 is a convenience store and Pearl Harbor is a grunge band from Seattle. That's because to know its significance would be to understand that everything their minds are being poisoned with in terms of "critical race theory" and "structural racism" is the titanic mega-mind-fuck to end all mind-fucks.[140]

As for the January 6 event at the Capitol that Biden stunningly called the worst attack since the Civil War, not a single person arrested was armed. The only person killed, Ashli Babbitt, was murdered by a member of the Capitol Police who to this day remains unnamed. That the FBI and DOJ have pretended those present that day were all domestic terrorists is a shocking turn of events. They've even placed some on a no-fly list, which is entirely unconstitutional. Their crimes were petty in comparison to the BLM/Antifa riots that destroyed numerous cities over the summer.

We all knew that Obama had weaponized all the federal agencies, from the IRS to the FBI, but now we

---

140 https://www.americanthinker.com/blog/2021/04/worst_attack_on_our_democracy_since_the_civil_war_can_biden_really_be_this_dumb.html

know just how far down the road to Marxism they've gone. We suffered a coup. How else do we explain the feds raiding Rudy Giuliani's residence but refusing to take the copy of Hunter Biden's laptop hard drive which is chock full of child porn among other disgusting things? Hunter Biden gets a job teaching at Tulane, and Rudy Giuliani is under investigation!

We are definitely not in Kansas anymore. We are fast becoming a facsimile of Mao's China or, when we see that vaccine passports may be required, Hitler's Germany. Biden is the dim and clueless tip of the spear of the Alinskyite Left's Trojan Horse. Unless the Republicans develop a collective spine, America and the freedoms guaranteed by our Constitution are soon to be gone.

Sadly, the fact that the timorous Republicans voted to confirm nearly every one of Biden's radical, racist cabinet appointees does not bode well for America's survival. They've put us at the mercy of an almost vicious anti-American left...

...No doubt millions of Americans who bothered to watch Biden's speech were horrified by his claim that the January 6 not-insurrection was the "worst attack on our democracy since the Civil War." It was an appalling statement, a monumental lie that betrayed

his administration's contempt for the American people. These people must be defeated.

The actual highlight of the night wasn't Biden but Senator Tim Scott's rebuttal and refutation of the poisonous bilge that emanated from the so-called quote-unquote "president's" filthy sewer. Most powerfully was his dismantling of the "Jim Crow" smearing of Georgia's new voter integrity laws as part of the genocidal blood-libeling of not just whites but decent people of every background, and his affirmation of the greatness of our founding:[141]

> *"Today, kids are being taught that the color of their skin defines them again — and if they look a certain way, they're an oppressor. From colleges to corporations to our culture, people are making money and gaining power by pretending we haven't made any progress at all, by doubling down on the divisions we've worked so hard to heal.*
>
> *You know this stuff is wrong. Hear me clearly: America is not a racist country. It's backwards to fight discrimination with different types of discrimination. And it's wrong to try to use our painful past to dishonestly shut down debates in the present...*

---

141 https://www.dailywire.com/news/tim-scott-shreds-joe-biden-in-rebuttal-speech-biden-is-tearing-us-apart-after-promising-to-unite-nation

...The state of Georgia passed a law that expands early voting; preserves no-excuse mail-in voting; and, despite what the president claimed, did not reduce Election Day hours. If you actually read this law, it's mainstream! It will be easier to vote early in Georgia than in Democrat-run New York.

Moving beyond the 100 days since Election Day 2020 and then into the first 100 days of the Biden junta, things are indeed getting darker all around us. Just *eight days afterwards came the untimely passing of Rush Limbaugh, who truly was "the voice of freedom, the voice of America."* [142] *The silencing of his voice puts an exclamation point on these events and serves as an incredibly powerful metaphor for the death of the republic.*

Since then, we've faced the intentional erasure of our borders, our freedoms, the rule of a just and stable law, our cultural heritage and our sanity. But there has been pushback, from some national political leaders (but far too few unfortunately), but most crucially from ordinary citizens. Citizens of a nation that as of last January ceased to exist, who are de facto internal exiles and what amounts to political prisoners of a hostile regime that grows more totalitarian by the day both as the reality that what they are promoting and doing come crashing down on their heads and that more and more people are rejecting the Kool Aid; either from the end of a syringe or over the airwaves. Somehow, some way, we find ourselves in some sort of nightmare alternate reality. When

---

142 htt ps://cutjibnewsletter.com/2021/02/18/the-morning-report-2-18-21/

even some intellectually honest diehard leftists like Naomi Wolf and Glenn Greenwald recognize this, you know we all got off at the wrong stop.

What is it going to take to reverse course? Day after day in writing my column, I come across essays where the authors, even some whom I greatly admire and regard as some of our best thinkers, while accurately identifying the problem offer no real solutions. All they suggest is the usual "organize," "stand up," "state your case" etc., and of course, "vote." On one of them, I commented:[143]

"Does the author not realize that the current junta consists of a nightmare regime that combines the worst elements of the Stasi controlling the government and Children of the Corn controlling the media and the private sector? When they declare all political opposition illegal and tantamount to treason - any day now I assume - then all of this talk of political organization let alone openly challenging people who support this is the equivalent of charging naked into a volcano."

As I threw up my hands in frustration, I thought, well, maybe in a sense the only choice is to take the plunge.[144]

143 https://amgreatness.com/2021/05/05/toward-a-national-liberation-movement/

144 https://dailycaller.com/2021/05/05/two-genders-louisiana-teacher-sounds-off-on-woke-education-school-board-meeting/

Jonathan Koeppel, a Louisiana high school teacher that went viral last month after objecting to his school's gender theory curriculum, spoke with the Daily Caller about his experience protesting the radical lessons.

Koeppel spoke out against gender identity education during an April school board meeting. Koeppel criticized an application used in school by students called "Brain Pop" for teaching about gender identity and personal pronouns.

"Who gave permission to talk about this? There's two genders," said Koeppel during the meeting. "I'm not going to work in a district that's okay with that."

I imagine Mr. Koeppel is going to have a shit ton of pressure on him to recant and renounce what he said and apologize or else lose his job – or be forced to put out the mostly peaceful flames on the backs of his children if he doesn't.

On a personal level, during dinner one night with a few friends, the conversation eventually turned to who got their vaccines, and when asked, I meekly said not yet. When pressed "well, when are you getting it," instead of just coming out and declaring I won't, I stammered something out and managed to change the subject. Not exactly a profile in courage, for which I now deeply regret.

Mr. Koeppel, just like the parents in Arizona who took over their school board meeting[145], or the barber in Michigan[146] who defied the shutdown orders of Wretched Whitmer[147] or ditto the California church that fought back against Gavin Newsom,[148] and so on, may all be isolated incidents, but they can't be merely outliers. Whether it's indoctrination, inoculation or incarceration for "insurrection" (spit), people are becoming scared, frustrated and angry. Are we voting our way out of this? More than likely not, given a whole host of reasons. Are we ultimately going to have to shoot our way out of this is the question. Perhaps not. But unlike me, it's going to take courage.

It's down to us. Each of us is going to have to be the Claudette Colvin[149], the Clarence Henderson[150], or the composite character of Virgil Hilts,[151] even if it means getting spit upon, beaten up, thrown into «the cooler» – or worse. Let's hope it never ever gets to that but I've seen enough and know enough to understand that it's better to die on your feet than merely exist on our knees.

---

145 https://www.thegatewaypundit.com/2021/04/angry-parents-take-arizona-school-district-board-meeting-protest-mask-mandate-children-cowardly-board-members-take-off-video/

146 https://pjmedia.com/news-and-politics/megan-fox/2020/05/22/michigan-barber-wins-in-court-against-gov-whitmer-health-department-failed-to-show-threat-n417195

147 Governor Gretchen Whitmer.

148 https://www.christianheadlines.com/contributors/michael-foust/supreme-court-gives-big-win-to-calif-churches-in-suit-against-worship-service-ban.html

149 https://www.womenshistory.org/articles/girl-who-acted-rosa-parks

150 https://nsjonline.com/article/2020/09/clarence-henderson-describes-path-from-1960-woolworths-sit-in-to-2020-featured-rnc-speech/

151 https://www.youtube.com/watch?v=IvJD3HUDYj4

Gradually, then all at once is how we got here. And I guess that's the way we'll ultimately get out of this. One by one. Be the revolution. One person. Then another and another and before you know it you're a force to be reckoned with. Pollyanna-ish? Maybe. But if we're going to wait around for the other guy to stick his neck out, we're dead already. Once again, it's Winston Churchill with the pearl of wisdom:

> *"If you will not fight for right when you can easily win without blood shed; if you will not fight when your victory is sure and not too costly;*
>
> *you may come to the moment when you will have to fight with all the odds against you and only a precarious chance of survival.*
>
> *There may even be a worse case. You may have to fight when there is no hope of victory, because it is better to perish than to live as slaves."*

* * * * *

Acknowledgements

In a nation that was founded principally on the bedrock of free speech, it's beyond tragic and bitterly ironic that I am forced to write under a pseudonym to protect myself and my loved ones from at the very least becoming societal outcasts to suffering actual physical harm. But that just underscores the theme of this book, insofar as the nation that I grew up in and cherished is no more. Still, there are friends and colleagues who rendered invaluable advice, counsel and support, and so must be recognized. Without them, this book would not have been possible.

— Ace, the co-bloggers and the commenters collectively known as "the Moron Horde" at Ace of Spades HQ for the opportunity to not only aggregate the day's news into "The Morning Report," but to editorialize and provide a platform for the smartest and funniest bunch in the blogosphere. In particular, to good friend, co-blogger and partner at our own site, CutJibNewsletter.com, Daniel Lapin. Thanks, bro.

— Thank you to Calamo Publishing for getting behind this book as well as being one of the few outlets for conservative (whatever the hell that word means these days), non-Leftist thought. Long may you wave.

— Priscilla Turner, one of my biggest boosters, for her outstanding work proof reading the manuscript and her sharp, critical eye. I know it was painful to revisit these days but I am truly grateful.

— Sabo, artist and visionary extraordinaire, for your incredible talent and passion in creating two signature masterpieces for the cover art, though only one made the cut. You are the Goya and Daumier of our age. Thank you!

— To my family -- especially my wife and my brother -- for all their love and support who, whether they know it or not, kept me going throughout.

Made in the USA
Monee, IL
11 November 2021

81894348R00156